"With his eye on current trends in the church, ar
adults, David Gushee throws a lifeline to all who
authentic, a return to Jesus' 'radical instruction' that calls Christians to
shape and renew their own lives—spiritual and social—while confronting
the challenges of a materialistic and increasingly amoral culture. The result
is a welcoming introduction to the teachings of the one whose moral vision
can still transform lives and cultures that will be ideal for both individual
and group study."

—R. ALAN CULPEPPER, dean and professor emeritus of New
Testament, McAfee School of Theology, Mercer University

"What does Jesus really say about how his followers should live? Clearing
the deck of polemical partisanship and free of cherry-picking soundbites
from Scripture, David Gushee guides us through the four Gospels and
shows us. He distills into forty succinct, reader-friendly, and academically
sound chapters Jesus' radical moral message for living in harmony with
God's ways. This book deserves a wide reading, not only among followers of
the Christian path, but of those who have grown weary of its many distortions in the public sphere."

—PETER ENNS, professor of biblical studies, Eastern University

"David Gushee offers us an insightful invitation to explore the principles
and practical implications of the teachings of Jesus afresh. This is a compelling and much needed new resource for our time! While it stands to engage
all who are curious about the teachings of Jesus, it's sure to equip the growing contingent of 'post-evangelical' Christians longing to embody a faithful
witness as they follow Jesus in our time."

—KERI LADOUCEUR, co-founder and executive
director, Post-Evangelical Collective

"David Gushee's *The Moral Teachings of Jesus* is an essential addition to the disciplines of Christian ethics *and* biblical scholarship. Gushee's engagement with the ethics of Jesus is a tour de force that invites the reader to radically reorder the ways that we engage the humanity of those that we often ignore. I look forward to assigning this text in my classes."

—**ANGELA N. PARKER**, associate professor of New Testament and Greek, McAfee School of Theology, Mercer University

"This book has been a long time coming. David Gushee is an ethicist, a pastor, and a follower of Jesus—who is taken, challenged, and sometimes baffled by the moral teachings of Jesus. In this compact yet comprehensive volume, one senses an existential attention to his subject. It is, in equal measure, illuminating and unsettling."

—**KEN WILSON**, pastor emeritus, Blue Ocean Church

"In this timely and important book, David Gushee presents a compelling exploration of the teachings and example of Jesus, emphasizing their enduring relevance and radical nature for justice, the flourishing of all creation, and the reality of peace. Gushee's insightful analysis invites contemporary seekers around the world to engage deeply with Jesus' example and teachings, especially at a time when ethical considerations and moral conflicts challenge the fabric of our societies. I found it challenging and transformative. I highly recommend it!"

—**DION A. FORSTER**, professor of public theology, Vrije Universiteit Amsterdam

"David Gushee—a crucial voice among theological ethicists—looks at familiar gospel stories with fresh eyes so as to interpret Jesus' moral teachings. Readable and accessible, Gushee seeks to counter the toxic Christianity prevalent among today's Christian nationalists by focusing on a Jesus who—along with so many today—reside on the margins."

—**MIGUEL A. DE LA TORRE**, professor of social
ethics and Latinx studies, Iliff School of Theology

"In *The Moral Teachings of Jesus*, David Gushee refocuses Christians on what matters most—the words and work of Christ. This book brings together a diverse variety of perspectives and theological disciplines in order to help the reader understand the words of Jesus in their fullness. I can't wait for this book to get in the hands of folks at our church. It is a game-changer."

—**ZACH W. LAMBERT**, lead pastor, Restore Austin

"In *Moral Teachings*, David Gushee has provided a gift to the church and the academy. Using the teachings of Jesus, other biblical passages, and learnings from historical figures, Gushee articulates a radical ethical understanding that provides a moral compass for our current context. This biblically sound, theologically astute, and ethically relevant book should be mandatory reading in classrooms, congregations, and other faith communities."

—**GRACE JI-SUN KIM**, professor of theology,
Earlham School of Religion

The Moral Teachings of Jesus

The Moral Teachings of Jesus

Radical Instruction in the Will of God

DAVID P. GUSHEE

CASCADE *Books* · Eugene, Oregon

THE MORAL TEACHINGS OF JESUS
Radical Instruction in the Will of God

Cascade Books
An Imprint of Wipf and Stock Publishers
199 W. 8th Ave., Suite 3
Eugene, OR 97401

www.wipfandstock.com

PAPERBACK ISBN: 978-1-6667-4476-7
HARDCOVER ISBN: 978-1-6667-4477-4
EBOOK ISBN: 978-1-6667-4478-1

Cataloguing-in-Publication data:

Names: Gushee, David P., author.

Title: The moral teachings of Jesus : radical instruction in the will of God / David P. Gushee.

Description: Eugene, OR: Cascade Books, 2024. Includes bibliographical references.

Identifiers: ISBN 978-1-6667-4476-7 (paperback) | ISBN 978-1-6667-4477-4 (hardcover) | ISBN 978-1-6667-4478-1 (ebook)

Subjects: LCSH: Jesus Christ—Teachings. | Jesus Christ—Ethics. | Christian ethics.

Classification: BJ1251 G86 2024 (paperback) | BJ1251 (ebook)

VERSION NUMBER 05/21/24

For my dear Jeanie—
partner in ministry and in life for forty years

Contents

Acknowledgments

My approach to interpreting the Bible, especially the teachings of Jesus, was shaped by the late Glen Stassen, who taught me a richly biblical version of Christian ethics at Southern Baptist Theological Seminary and became my dear mentor, co-author, and friend. I acknowledge his great influence here.

These Gospel texts were worked over carefully by the inaugural "Moral Teachings of Jesus" class at Mercer University's School of Theology, spring 2023. I express my gratitude to each student for their classroom discussions, exegesis papers, and sermons. That fine class included Steve Baker, Jeremy Ball, Jasyn Banks, Audrey Brown, Bob Brown, Bryant Culpepper, Will Cumbia, Tricia Etheridge, Averee Gentry, Kristen Godsey, Ashley Guthas, Dustin Heitman, Mia Hong, Shelby Howard, Sarah Lewis, Douglas Mathis, Emily Niehoff, Jamila Smith, Carie Whitaker, and Terri Womack.

I want to thank my protégé and friend Jeremy S. Hall for his partnership in guiding that first Moral Teachings class, his close attention to these Gospel texts, and careful contribution to the exegetical work. I am also very grateful to New Testament scholar Amy-Jill Levine, and pastors Ken Wilson and Don Schiewer, for their many helpful comments on the manuscript.

I acknowledge with gratitude the invaluable line-by-line editorial suggestions offered by my wife, Jeanie, always my best editor. If this is the last book, we have ended well.

Of course, in the end, the author always bears full responsibility for the final work.

Introduction

THE CURRENT MOMENT REVEALS many people, especially young adults, leaving the churches in which they were raised. Some are forming or participating in new churches—for example, in the exciting post-evangelical movement of which I am now a part.[1] Others, however, are leaving church altogether.

So many of those who are leaving are doing so because they have concluded that aspects of their faith tradition are no longer healthy. They feel a theological vacuum at best, and toxicity at worst, that in some cases is driving them right out of church. Their churches no longer seem to have much to do with the Jesus whom they are supposed to be about.

Just go onto social media (if you dare) and watch Christians argue over the most basic issues, including the very meaning of Christianity, the gospel, or the Bible. It is astonishing to see especially toxic posts in which articulations of the teachings of Jesus are derided, by "Christians," as a form of weakness. This is toxic masculinity and Nietzschean will to power masquerading as Christianity.

But it is not only the dissidents and departers who are (or ought to be) looking for a fresh encounter with the teachings of Jesus. Surely any time is the right time, and any church is the right church, to seek the spiritual and moral renewal that comes from close study of the astonishing, bracing, demanding moral teachings of Jesus.

To bring Christians back to first principles, and to offer resources to all sectors of the church today, in this book I will examine all four New Testament (NT) Gospels to attend closely to what Jesus said about how his followers should live.

1. Check out the Post-Evangelical Collective, which I serve as a theological advisor: Post-Evangelical Collective (postevangelicalcollective.org)

It has been quite a while since a focused treatment of the moral teachings of Jesus has been attempted in Christian ethics.[2] Overall, Paul's moral teaching rather than that of Jesus has received more attention both by pastors and scholars in recent decades. It appears that the Social Gospel movement, over one hundred years ago, was the last era in which works centered on Jesus' moral teachings were common.[3] How desperately we need a return to a focus on the teachings of Jesus.

I am aiming for a brisk, readable survey for preachers/homilists, Bible teachers in homes, schools, and churches, and regular Christians as well as interested seekers. Each chapter offers the needed exegetical work to address textual and linguistic issues that might affect the interpretation of a passage. Relevant related passages are noted, and biblical commentaries are cited and sometimes quoted for expanded coverage of issues. These chapters stay tightly focused on the moral teachings and implications of the text/s in question. The chapters are not sermons, but they ought to be helpful for anyone responsible for preaching and teaching not just what Jesus' instruction *meant* at the time but what it might now be *taken to mean*.

The Gospels of Matthew (Matt) and Luke offer the greatest moral treasures, simply by sheer volume of content, but I also consider the ethical content of Mark and John. Indeed, Mark is central for reasons I will explain just below. This book does not comment on the whole text of each Gospel but on passages that clearly offer moral instruction, at least in my view. Where there are parallel texts, they are treated together, only commenting on notable differences. The reader is encouraged to read the full version of all passages before tackling my exposition.

Two presuppositions at work in this book, widely shared by biblical scholars, are 1) that Jesus' moral teachings were circulated as sayings for decades before being edited and integrated into the narratives offered by the Gospel writers, and 2) that Mark was the first completed written Gospel. This book tries to focus on the core moral teaching of Jesus, letting the chronology start with the version offered by Mark, with consideration of parallels in the other Gospels. Only after Mark's renderings of Jesus' moral

---

2. Christian ethics is the academic discipline that describes, analyzes, and proposes moral norms for Christian character and behavior. Biblical scholars have produced studies of the teachings of Jesus, but Christian ethics brings a different lens to bear on this subject.

3. A good example: Walter Rauschenbusch, *Social Principles of Jesus*, as well as several of his other works. Rauschenbusch is a model for me in his serious engagement with the teachings of Jesus.

teachings are exhausted do I move to the texts found not in Mark but only in the other Gospels. Thus, the treatment of texts in this book is in this order: Mark, Matthew, Luke, John. The one exception to this approach is that I have saved three narratives tied to Jesus' last week of life as our last passages to consider. Of course, readers are free to jump in anywhere.

My approach assumes that these core teachings were in fact offered by Jesus—more precisely, these sayings *were circulated by the early church as teachings of Jesus.* I want to try to respect these Jesus sayings as they existed before the Gospel writers edited and positioned them. It is true, of course, that this somewhat de-emphasizes the specific Gospels as literary creations and instead emphasizes the teachings of Jesus as they circulated in the early church, but that is not an unreasonable choice. Still, we will watch for the edits made by each Gospel writer, in part to understand what each made of the teaching of Jesus as a part of their own theological work.

In terms of research sources, besides a handful of Bible commentaries,[4] I have invited along a diverse group of fellow interpreters for the ride. They include as our Bible text the *Jewish Annotated New Testament* (JANT), a unique study Bible edited by Jewish NT scholars,[5] NT scholar Brian Blount's edited volume in African American biblical studies called *True to Our Native Land,* NT scholar Love Lazarus Secrest's womanist text called *Race and Rhyme,* mid-twentieth-century German theologian Dietrich Bonhoeffer's *Discipleship,* Christian ethicist Miguel De La Torre's *The Politics of Jesús,* Jewish NT scholar Amy Jill-Levine's *Short Stories of Jesus,* mid-twentieth-century theologian Howard Thurman's *Jesus and the Disinherited,* the *Women's Bible Commentary,* and the *Kingdom Ethics* textbook that Glen Stassen and I wrote together.[6] This list reflects certain key commitments: to do serious exegetical work (including attention to the Greek text), to engage seriously the first-century Jewish Jesus, to avoid destructive historic patterns of antisemitic readings

4. Edwards, *Gospel According to Mark*; Garland, *NIV Application Commentary: Mark*; Davies and Allison, Jr., *Matthew*; Culpepper, *Matthew*; Gadenz, *Gospel of Luke*; Green, *Gospel of Luke*; Ford, *Gospel of John*; Morris, *Gospel According to John*; Thompson, *John*.

5. JANT uses the NRSV. Recently, the NRSV was very lightly updated to become the NRSVue. This is the English translation I will cite unless otherwise indicated.

6. Levine and Brettler, eds., *Jewish Annotated New Testament* (henceforth abbreviated as JANT); Blount, gen. ed., *True to Our Native Land*; Secrest, *Race and Rhyme*; Bonhoeffer, *Discipleship*; De La Torre, *Politics of Jesús*; Levine, *Short Stories of Jesus*; Thurman, *Jesus and the Disinherited*; Lapsley, Newsom, and Ringe, *Women's Bible Commentary*; Gushee and Stassen, *Kingdom Ethics*.

of the NT, and to learn from the insights offered by writers hailing from a wide variety of social locations other than my own.

The category "moral teachings" denotes teachings intended to instruct Jesus' listeners, especially his committed disciples, about God's moral will for their character and behavior. Yet *Jesus taught through his life, not just his words.* When Jesus fed the hungry, cured the sick, cast out demons, and dined with "sinners," he was teaching. With just a handful of exceptions, I have not treated such events of Jesus' ministry as teachings, so as not to lose my intended focus on the often-evaded actual teachings of Jesus.

I considered growing this book to offer sections focused on the moral implications of Jesus' death and resurrection, but I decided that there is value in a tight focus on the verbal teachings of Jesus themselves. It is easy for Christians to ignore these teachings because we become so transfixed by the central events of Holy Week. This book wants to do something different, without in any way obviating the significance of Jesus' cross and resurrection.

I settled on a grand total of forty "pericopes"—individual and/or parallel moral teachings of Jesus. There were some judgment calls here, in terms of which teachings were included and excluded from the "moral" category. So that the book could be both thorough and of reasonable length, I aimed for a range of 1,500 to 1,600 words per chapter. This forced me to distill what could be said about each passage to the very essence of what this Christian ethicist, at least, believes is most important. I hope you enjoy this journey into the moral teachings of Jesus, whom we will see throughout these pages offered radical instruction in the will of God.

PART ONE

Mark

1

The Kingdom of God

Now after John was arrested, Jesus came to Galilee proclaiming the good news of God and saying, "The time is fulfilled, and the kingdom of God has come near; repent, and believe in the good news."

—MARK 1:14–15

He put before them another parable: "The kingdom of heaven is like a mustard seed that someone took and sowed in his field; it is the smallest of all the seeds, but when it has grown it is the greatest of shrubs and becomes a tree, so that the birds of the air come and make nests in its branches."

—MATT 13:31–32

Texts: Mark 1:14–15/Matt 4:12–17,[1] cf. Luke 4:14–30, Matt 13:24–50

JESUS BEGAN HIS MINISTRY by announcing that "the kingdom of God (*basileia tou theou*) has come near" (Mark 1:15). It was clearly an electrifying message.

---

1. Passages marked like the above, with a slash, indicate that they are formally parallel texts; "cf." here means, please compare the connected or related passages then listed.

Jesus' proclamation resembled and built upon the message of his immediate forerunner, the prophet John the Baptist (Mark 1:2–8). Not overidentifying the two, it is still instructive to see what the contemporaneous John the Baptist does with his proclamation.

John offers a warning of imminent divine wrath (Matt 3:7), a baptismal ministry associated with repentance and preparation for judgment day, and a claim that "one who is more powerful than I is coming after me" to bring this judgment to fruition (Matt 3:11–12). Throngs of people recognized this simultaneously forbidding and attractive desert figure as a prophet of God and were baptized by him. His ministry ended with his arrest (Mark 1:14) and later his wanton execution at the hands of King Herod and his family (Mark 6:14–29 and parallels).

After John's arrest (Mark 1:14), Jesus began his own public ministry by proclaiming the kingdom of God. The Gospel writers never show Jesus explicating a precise formula as to what he meant by this phrase, which has made this crucial concept a matter of scholarly debate, and vulnerable to ignorance and misunderstanding.

There is some content visible in Jesus' proclamation of the kingdom as recorded in the NT. We see him returning to the phrase time and again, in parables and sayings. Look especially at Matt 13:24–50.[2] (Due to its unique significance for ethics, we will isolate Matt 13:24–30, 36–43 in a later chapter.)

The passage opens with the kingdom of God depicted as a *mustard seed* (13:31–32)—it starts with a very small beginning, and ends with a great outcome, in a process that God alone has set in motion. Then there is the kingdom as *a bit of yeast* (13:33), mixed in with three measures of flour (that's a lot), leavening the whole dough, which may also symbolize permeation and massive expansion from a small beginning. Next we find the kingdom as a *treasure hidden in a field* and as a *pearl of great price*, the one thing worth more than anything else (13:44–46).[3] Finally, Jesus offers

---

2. Note that Matt uses the phrase "kingdom of heaven" rather than "kingdom of God." Scholars believe that this was probably to avoid uttering the holy name of God—a specifically Jewish emphasis. The meaning of the two phrases should not be differentiated.

3. Levine, *Short Stories of Jesus*, chs. 3–5, offers extensive and creative reflections on these three images for the kingdom and what they might be taken to mean. The pearl story helps us in "challenging our acquisitiveness and our sense of what is truly of value" (164); the stories of the mustard seed and yeast in the dough, may be taken to refer to something small growing naturally to produce great effects that benefit many (181), that each illustrates "potential that needs to be actualized" (182), and that this potential is best actualized if after we get it going we leave it alone and get out of the way (182). Levine

us the kingdom as like a net full of fish, sorted out into categories of good and bad, representing the final sorting out of the evil and the just at the end of the age (13:47–50). These presentations carry an air of mystery, growth, grandeur, and divine power. They invite listeners to want to be a part of the great thing God is doing.

If we take Luke 4:14–30 as Luke's expanded version of Jesus' initial kingdom message, we get even more content. Here Jesus chooses and quotes Isa 61 and claims it for himself. Jesus is the anointed one who brings good news to the poor, proclaims release to the captives, recovery of sight to the blind, and freedom for the oppressed. Jesus is the one who announces "the year of the Lord's favor," sometimes connected by interpreters to the Jubilee promise from OT law (Lev 25), but just as easily connected to the kingdom of God.

Jesus' kingdom message "announces an event, the coming of God's new world,"[4] which is *good news,* more than John the Baptist's message seemed to be. Like John, Jesus speaks of wrath, but Jesus also speaks of God's mercy, of God's *deliverance,* especially for those mistreated in this age before God's intervention.

The kingdom of God was a concept derived from the Hebrew Bible's very basic claim that God is King, not just of Israel but all the earth.[5] For examples drawn from the Psalms, see Pss 5, 47, 74, 93, 95, 97, 99; for examples from the prophets, see Isa 44:6, Jer 10:10, Ezek 20:33, and Dan 4:34 and 6:26.

The basic idea is that not only is there one true God above all the other gods vainly worshipped in this world, but there is also one true King above all the earthly kings vainly parading their permanence, pomp, and power.[6] Even Israel's kings were to be disciplined in their behavior and self-understanding by the idea that God alone is true King—and sometimes they were indeed constrained by this crucial idea. A key part of the prophetic calling was to remind Israel's kings who was truly King of Israel.

The idea of God's rightful reign over all the earth was sharpened and made plaintive by the experience of the Jewish people's suffering at the

---

also emphasizes that the homey/homely setting for these examples emphasizes that the kingdom happens in "our own backyard" (182), not somewhere grand and far away.

4. Garland, *Mark,* 59.

5. I have offered an exposition of the meaning of the kingdom of God both in *Kingdom Ethics,* with Glen Stassen, and in my more recent *Introducing Christian Ethics.* Gushee/Stassen, *Kingdom Ethics,* ch. 1; Gushee, *Introducing Christian Ethics,* ch. 5.

6. Edwards, *Mark,* 46.

hands of foreign tyrants. Brokenhearted Israel asserted, while in the direst straits—*the God of Israel is king of all the earth*! Such a proclamation by Jews while in foreign lands, or in their own land under foreign domination—as in first-century CE Roman-occupied Judea—was intrinsically subversive and could be perceived as revolutionary.

The story that is being told underneath all kingdom-of-God proclamation is that this world is in rebellion against God, its rightful king. This rebellion merits God's judgment. But the good news, especially emphasized by Jesus, is that God coming as King means God coming to deliver those crushed by this world's cruel kings and kingdoms. A prophet could emphasize either the judgment dimension of the coming kingdom of God (as John the Baptist did), or the mercy dimension, or both dimensions (as Jesus did).

The kingdom of God is a *theological* teaching in the sense that it reaffirms God's Kingship, God's rightful sovereign rule, over not just Israel, but all the world.

The kingdom is an *eschatological* teaching insofar as the kingdom is an event of the end of time, which is beginning right now. NT scholar David Garland writes: "The future created by God is no longer a flickering hope . . . it has become available in the present."[7]

The kingdom is a *teaching about the character and activity of God in the world*, insofar as Jesus proclaims that a redeemed world looks like salvation, deliverance, justice, peace, healing, and a restored and remade covenant community. As *True to Our Native Land*, an African American NT commentary, puts it: "God's imperial reign is more about a holistic, societal, communal transformation than about individual salvation. . . . This vision . . . requires a restructuring of the sociopolitical standing of those on the margins."[8]

The kingdom is a *moral teaching for followers of Jesus* because our response to, and readiness for, the dawning kingdom is part of what Jesus is intending to teach. "The divine rule blazed abroad by Jesus . . . requires immediate human decision and commitment."[9] Disciples of Jesus are defined by obediently participating in what God is doing by our acts of deliverance, justice, peace, compassion, healing, and restored community. The concept of the kingdom of God thus gives followers of Jesus their behavioral marching orders.

---

7. Garland, *Mark*, 60.

8. Emerson Powery, "Gospel of Mark," in Blount, *True to Our Native Land*, 122.

9. Garland, *Mark*, 60.

In the kingdom-of-God idea we have powerful motivation for moral actions in this world, and many Christians indeed have been motivated by it to strenuous acts of compassion and justice.

But the concept is vulnerable to various distortions. If pushed entirely into the future, it can fail to serve as present motivation. If robbed of human co-participation with God, it can create passivity before divine sovereignty.[10] If expected too imminently, it can forestall efforts that require a longer time horizon. If identified too closely with this world's policies, occurrences, or regimes, it can create an unhealthy confusion of God's redemptive activity with human events and earthly politics.

It also must be noted that the very idea of a "kingdom" is monarchical and male-centered language that may not help us get beyond undemocratic and patriarchal thinking, which we do need to get beyond. "Kin-dom" is an interesting alternative, emphasizing the inclusive-familial nature of Jesus' understanding of what "kingdom community" should look like.

The kingdom of God was "the substance of Jesus' teaching."[11] According to the Synoptic Gospels (Matt, Mark, Luke), it is where Jesus himself started as he launched his ministry. That is why it is where we start this treatment of what can be described as the grand story, the theological vision, and the essential core of the moral teachings of Jesus.

---

10. Here I dissent from Edwards, *Mark*, 46, when he says, "The kingdom of God is not a result of human effort." I believe Jesus teaches discipleship as co-participation with God in kingdom work.

11. Edwards, *Mark*, 46.

2

Sabbath Observance

Then he said to them, "The Sabbath was made for humankind and not humankind for the Sabbath, so the Son of Man is lord even of the Sabbath."

—MARK 2:27-28

Texts: Mark 2:23—3:6/Matt 12:1-14/Luke 6:1-11

A CORE FEATURE OF narratives about Jesus is the "controversy story." Jesus goes about his ministry, saying and doing things that evoke controversy and opposition. Just working with Mark for the moment, in the order in which they appear the primary foils who oppose Jesus are scribes (Mark 2:6), Pharisees (Mark 2:16), Herodians (Mark 3:6), chief priests (Mark 11:18), elders (Mark 11:27), and Sadducees (Mark 12:18). By Mark 8 Jesus is already predicting that the chief priests, elders, and scribes will reject him and take actions leading to his execution (Mark 8:31).

Let's consider this cast of characters. The Pharisees were deeply devout adherents of Jewish Law, notable for their teaching that all Jews ought to live according to the entirety of Torah, including the requirements prescribed for the priests. They were respected for their piety and knowledge of the Law. Their acceptance of traditions and practices that went beyond the written Torah proved controversial at the time, but eventually became the mainstream position, and proved essential in the survival of Judaism under varied, difficult post-biblical circumstances.

The Sadducees were members of the Sanhedrin, a governing body set up to handle Jewish affairs. Other members of the Sanhedrin included the high priests and the elders. These latter two groups were particularly concerned with the place of the temple in the life of the people. All three groups were seen by some frustrated Jewish nationalists as colluding with the Roman occupiers. Another group of power players that make up the common cast of Jesus' opponents were the Herodians. These were mostly wealthy aristocrats who had allied with the Herodian dynasty (client kingdom of the Roman Empire) for the sake of stability and their bottom line.

These various figures were all Jews. They performed different roles in first-century Jewish life and represented conflicting parties and beliefs. Some of them did not survive the Jewish-Roman War of 66–70 CE. But as framed in the Gospel narratives, written a generation or more later, the details don't really matter all that much. They are Jewish leaders of various types, and they most often challenge Jesus.

It must be noted here that this framing of Jesus vs. "various Jewish leaders," so pervasive in the Gospels, helped fuel centuries of Christian contempt toward Jews and Judaism, a destructive interpretive tradition that must be rejected. Amy-Jill Levine, a Jewish scholar of the New Testament, has taken a leading role in challenging antisemitism/anti-Judaism in Christian biblical interpretation. The *Jewish Annotated New Testament* (abbreviated here as JANT), for which she served as a co-editor, is one key example of her immense contribution.[1]

An early subject of controversy in Mark's Gospel has to do with the observance of the Jewish Sabbath. In Mark 2:23–28, the trigger is when Jesus' hungry disciples begin to pluck heads of grain to eat while wandering through grainfields on the Sabbath. In the next story, Mark 3:1–6, Jesus heals a man in a synagogue on the Sabbath. Even though he does not touch him, his verbal healing triggers such anger that Pharisees and Herodians already begin conspiring "how to destroy him" (Mark 3:6). These stories are repeated in pretty much identical form in Matt 12:1–14 and Luke 6:1–11.

---

1. The copious notes and essays in JANT are an important part of its contribution and will be cited periodically here. These notes come from several scholars, while the overall work, as noted above, is edited by Levine and Marc Zvi Brettler.

There are several Greek words that the author of Mark could have chosen in Mark 3:6.

- *apokteinō*—This word generally means "to kill outright" or "to put to death" and is often used in reference to execution or murder.

- *thanatoō*—This word means "to cause to die" and is often used in a broader sense to refer to death in general.

- *sphazō*—This word means "to slaughter" and is often used in reference to the killing of animals for sacrifice or consumption.

- *anaireō*—This word means "to take away" or "to destroy" and is often used in a more figurative sense to refer to the ending of something, such as a person's life or a plan.

- *kteinō*—This word means "to slay" or "to kill" and is often used in reference to violent death or murder.

However, the word the author chooses is *apollumi*, which is more akin to English phrases like "to utterly destroy" or "to ruin." It appears to be the most powerful available Greek word. Jesus must be *crushed*. We need to try to understand why his actions evoked such a powerfully negative reaction, at least according to Mark.

Both the issue of Jesus' disciples plucking grain on the Sabbath to have something to eat (Mark 2:23–28), and the healing of a man with a withered hand (Mark 3:1–6), are focused fundamentally on the interpretation of Sabbath prohibitions against work. The blessing of the seventh day as a day of rest and worship is introduced in the Genesis narrative (Gen 2:2–3) and is included in both versions of the Ten Commandments (Exod 20:8–11, Deut 5:12–15). It is one of Judaism's most holy and distinctive blessings— and obligations.

Various interpretations of precisely what constitutes violating the command to rest by working on the Sabbath, and whether there can be exceptions, inevitably emerged in Judaism.

The Talmud, the central text of rabbinic Judaism and the authoritative treatment of Jewish religious law, consists primarily of commentaries on the Hebrew Bible that were developed before, during, and for a few centuries after the time of Jesus. Writings in the Talmud, often cited in JANT, can shed light on rabbinic debates on issues also addressed by Jesus.

For example, the Tosefta, a compilation of early rabbinic legal traditions generally dated to the late second century CE, includes a provision for setting aside Sabbath prohibitions to save a life (*t.Shabb.* 16:12). So that idea was accepted, or at least, it was argued. But in neither of these cases was Jesus saving a life. He was permitting the work required to get a bit of food for hungry mouths, and then healing a man. However wonderful that healing was for the man in question, could it not have waited a day?

The core statements of principle that Jesus offers in Mark 2:27–28 are "The Sabbath was made for humankind, not humankind for the Sabbath," and "The Son of Man is lord even of the Sabbath." And then there is also what he says in the synagogue: "Is it lawful to do good or to do harm on the Sabbath, to save life or to kill?" (Mark 3:4).

The first statement resonates with a key original rationale for the Sabbath—so that animals and humans would have a day of rest from their unrelenting labors, which in the Hebrew Bible is tied to the primal experience of enslavement under the Egyptians (Deut 5:12–15). Sabbath is a gift from God for rest.

The second statement may mean that Jesus is claiming messianic authority to redefine Sabbath obligation, which would have been shocking to his listeners and inevitably would have aroused their opposition. This is the most common Christian interpretation.[2]

It is possible, though, that Jesus was simply affirming that human beings are "lords" of the Sabbath in terms of needing the freedom to interpret the day's blessings and demands in terms of deeper well-being concerns. A key issue has to do with how to interpret the phrase "son of humankind" (*hyios ho anthrōpos*), usually translated by Christians as "Son of Man," and traditionally tied to a messianic reading of the eschatological scene in Dan 7:13–14.[3]

But see how different the phrase reads if the caps are taken away and it is read as "son of man," that is, "child of humans," which means simply, *human being*. This would point toward a democratized, humanistic, maybe even liberative interpretation: that people need to be in charge of their practice of the Sabbath so that it meets its deepest intended purpose.[4]

There is a problem, though. If Sabbath observance is relativized to the point that people are free to do anything that they believe amounts to doing

---

2. Edwards, *Mark*, 97; Garland, *Mark*, 106.

3. The position taken by Edwards, *Mark*, 97.

4. "It is not only the Son of Man who had authority over the Sabbath but *all* humans *also* do . . . African Americans . . . have depended on this freedom of action on the Sabbath." Powery, "The Gospel of Mark," in Blount, *True to Our Native Land*, 126. Italics in the original. This position is explicitly rejected by Edwards, *Mark*, 97.

some good for human well-being, then Sabbath obligations and indeed, Sabbath blessings, might well be relativized into nonexistence.[5] The fundamental purposes of Sabbath—worship of God and rest from labor—might be washed away by other priorities.

Overall, the question of the nature and power of religious-moral commands must be taken seriously. This is especially true in Christian circles that tend more toward antinomianism (law/rule-free religion, in which human intuition and divine grace govern the understanding of morality) than toward legalism (hyper-attention to binding and obligatory religious laws/rules, applied with excessive strictness).

If we focus on the divine *command* rather than the *purpose* for which the command was given, we can end up with the worst result of legalism, which is to do harm to people in the name of obeying God's commands. But if we focus so much on the purpose of a command that we attenuate its binding power, its strength as a command can evaporate, and we can end up with the worst result of antinomianism, which is a lack of clear and binding moral obligations.

Looking around at most Christians today, is it fair to say that Sabbath observance for worship and rest is treated as a binding obligation? Might we acknowledge that the protections from overwork that were offered by the binding Sabbath command in Judaism have been weakened out of existence, both in religion and in economic life, in our antinomian versions of Christianity?

Any observer of the lives of the overworked laborer juggling three jobs knows the answer to this question. While recognizing the profound issues about the relationship between Law and human well-being that Jesus raises here, it certainly seems that today the need is for a stronger rather than weaker commitment to the concept of a Sabbath for people to rest and, if they choose, to turn their hearts to the God who made them.

---

5. That is the problem with the distressingly familiar antinomianism in an interpretive move like this one, by David Garland: "The priority of human need always outweighs the need for humans to conform to ritual formalities" (Garland, *Mark*, 107).

3

Family Problems

A crowd was sitting around him, and they said to him, "Your mother and your brothers are outside asking for you." And he replied, "Who are my mother and my brothers?" And looking at those who sat around him, he said, "Here are my mother and my brothers! Whoever does the will of God is my brother and sister and mother."

—MARK 3:32–35

Texts: Mark 3:20–35/Matt 12:46–50/Luke 8:19–21, cf. Matt 10:34–37, Luke 14:26

AT THE CATHOLIC CHURCH that I attend with my wife in Atlanta, when you look up at the altar you see three statues affixed to the back wall. On the left is Mary, dressed in her traditional blue and white. On the right is a middle-aged Joseph, holding his hammer. And of course, at the center is Jesus on the cross.

There they are, Mary, Jesus, and Joseph, the Holy Family, in sublime unity. But the Gospels present us evidence that all was not always well in the Holy Family. Mark, which we have noted appears to have been the first Gospel account to be written, offers by far the most extensive account of the state of the grown-up Jesus' relationship with his family. It is placed very near the beginning of Jesus' ministry, right after his selection of the twelve apostles. That may be significant—perhaps it is precisely when Jesus has selected a new kind of family to accompany him on his high-stakes, high-conflict itinerant ministry that his "old" family feels the need to intervene.

In the first part of the passage in Mark 3:20–35, Jesus goes to his hometown and is swarmed by crowds. So: "His family went out to restrain him" (Mark 3:21). It is of note that there are ten Greek words that can be translated to "seize, grab, restrain, arrest" but the one that Mark uses is *krateō*, which is the same word used when Jesus is forcibly arrested in the garden of Gethsemane. The word carries with it an air of authority, like how the police or the state can *krateō* you.[1] Exercising parental-familial authority, they want to "arrest" Jesus and take him home.

The family's concern was that "people were saying" that "he has gone out of his mind" (Mark 3:21).[2] At that moment scribes from Jerusalem pile on to say that Jesus is possessed by Satan. No gap exists within the text between these accusations. Family members are worried about their Jesus, the neighbors say he's crazy, and the scribes suggest "he has Beelzebul."

The use of the term *Beelzebul* is interesting, in that they used this proper noun instead of "the devil," "a demon," or "Satan." Beelzebul is from the name Ba'al and carries with it implications of blasphemy and idol worship.[3] There is some subtext here, a secondary layer of implication to this term that might reveal some of what the scribes are actually accusing him of. A tough day in Nazareth!

Jesus appears to be truly offended by the accusation of demon-possession. In Mark, this is where Jesus declares that it makes no sense to accuse an exorcist of being possessed by Satan. "How can Satan cast out Satan?" (3:23). Jesus goes on to say that blasphemy against the Holy Spirit—which is what this accusation amounts to—is *the* unforgivable sin (3:29).

The family arrives and tries to get to him. *Hey, Jesus, your family is outside and wants to see you.* It is at that moment that he offers a response that can be seen as one of his most shocking statements: "Who are my mother and my brothers?" He looks at his family, and then he looks at the receptive crowd gathered at his feet, and says to the latter, "Here are my mother and

---

1. Garland, *Mark*, 130.

2. This shocking accusation, especially in the context of Jesus and his family, is omitted in the Matt and Luke parallels. Edwards, *Mark*, 118.

3. Edwards, *Mark*, 120.

my brothers! Whoever does the will of God is my brother and sister and mother" (3:33–35).[4]

In Luke 14, Jesus takes it a shocking step further: "Whoever comes to me and does not hate father and mother, wife and children, brothers and sisters, yes, and even life itself, cannot be my disciple" (Luke 14:26).

This is just *not* what religious leaders say, and it is not the kind of statement that any known culture blesses. It would not go over well in my family. It would not go over well in any family. Is this a "moral teaching of Jesus," in the sense that here is an instruction for how his followers are supposed to live their lives? Not too many mothers and fathers would be very enthusiastic about that. Indeed, I can think of many cults in which precisely this happens—adherents are taught to regard their fellow cultists as their new family, and to cut their old family off, even "hate" them, if necessary.

In terms of the trajectory of the early ministry of Jesus in Mark, look at what he has already done—he has evoked opposition not only from every sector of religious leadership in the Jewish community, but also from his neighbors in his hometown, and now from his family. All he has left now is his new ragtag community of followers.

He also has his God, the God who is his real Father, the God who has blessed him at his baptism with an affirmation of his Sonship and has anointed him with the Holy Spirit (Mark 1:9–11).[5] In radical relation to God his Father, Jesus is Son, and others who are radically committed to doing God's will are his new sisters and brothers. Jesus has redefined family vertically, and thus redefined family altogether.

If this is a moral teaching, and not just an expression unique to Jesus the only Son of God, perhaps it can be expressed in this way: *no human being or human community deserves ultimate allegiance—not even blood relatives.* If we truly believe in the God taught about and revealed by Jesus, then we know that this God is the only one worthy of ultimate allegiance; indeed, that it is not just folly but spiritually dangerous to offer such allegiance to anyone else. It is this God who created us, sustains us, and redeems us. It is

4. Powery, "Gospel of Mark," in Blount, *True to Our Native Land*, 128, notes that Jesus adds "sisters" himself, thus "providing direct approval of female participation in doing the will of God." Edwards, *Mark*, 125, notes that Jesus leaves "father" out, perhaps because Joseph has died, perhaps because "no one except God can be called Father by Jesus."

5. I use the "Father" and "Son" language advisedly but intentionally, because it was clearly Jesus' own language and because editing it in this context for gender inclusivity obscures that.

this God from whom we came and to whom we shall return when we die. It is this God whose reign over all the earth must be acknowledged by all flesh, one way or another (Phil 2:5–11).

In those fortunate circumstances in which our families share with us this kind of commitment to God's kingdom, there need be no conflict between these loyalties. Jesus is not anti-family, but pro-reign-of-God.[6] Garland writes: "One's ultimate devotion is owed to God, who is head of a new divine family."[7] We can see in the book of Acts that after his resurrection and ascension Jesus' mother and brothers have come around to full participation in his movement (Acts 1:14). That's great news. But many readers will know of situations in which it has come down to a choice between loyalty to the will of an earthly family and loyalty to the will of God. This teaching stiffens the spine. It prepares us for that choice if it should come to it.

In his classic 1937 book *Discipleship*, written during the disastrous Nazi era in Germany, Dietrich Bonhoeffer made two statements about this passage that are worth considering. Here is the first: "Christ makes everyone he calls into an individual. Each is called alone. Each must follow alone."[8] And then this: "Everyone enters discipleship alone, but no one remains alone in discipleship."[9] Sometimes we avoid real personal encounter with Christ by falling back into the arms of family and other relationships of this life. Christ's words here challenge that path. But they also comfort, in this way—on this journey, we will not be alone. We will have our fellow disciples, and Christ himself.

6. Powery, "Gospel of Mark," in Blount, *True to Our Native Land*, 128.

7. Garland, *Mark*, 131.

8. Bonhoeffer, *Discipleship*, 92. I note here that despite his brilliance, and devotion to Christ, Bonhoeffer reflected his era insofar as he attempted to think theologically about Jews and Judaism, and his work is to be read with caution on that front.

9. Bonhoeffer, *Discipleship*, 99.

4

Tradition

You abandon the commandment of God and hold to human tradition.
—*Mark 7:8*

Texts: Mark 7:1–23/Matt 15:1–20

In this passage, Jesus is criticized by Pharisees and some of the scribes for not requiring that his disciples practice their version of Jewish ritual purity practice, beginning with handwashing and extending to how kitchen objects and perhaps food were ritually purified (Mark 7:2–4). Jesus' supposed abandonment of the "tradition of the elders" (Mark 7:5) here had to do not strictly with Torah observance but with Pharisaic innovations that were not universally accepted in the Jewish community.[1] These innovations were intended to protect Jewish identity and to make Torah provisions apply to all, rather than just ot the priests in the temple—but they could also be interpreted as adding questionable rules to biblical Law. (This has been known to happen in other religious traditions as well, including conservative Christianity. Old-time Baptists used to ban dancing, so as not to trigger desires for illicit sex. My late father, a former Baptist, used to say that his church banned illicit sex so as not to trigger desires for dancing.)

1. Lawrence M. Wills, notes to "The Gospel According to Mark," in JANT, 84.

Jesus responds sharply, by quoting Isa 29:13 to cast his critics as "hypocrites" (Mark 7:6) with only the appearance of true righteousness, and as those who have abandoned God's command to substitute human tradition (Mark 7:8). The example Jesus gives of this is his claim that his critics have abrogated the clear teaching to honor their parents when they have made vow offerings to God. The basic problem seems to be that support for elderly parents has been sacrificed to a Corban-type vow, in which an item is declared devoted to God through an irrevocable vow. Jesus treats the latter as a human tradition that is "making void the word of God" (7:13) because it ends up dishonoring parents.

This is best understood as a case in which two positive obligations of Torah (and not just Pharisaic tradition) might end up conflicting with each other. Those two obligations are to honor parents (Exod 20:12, Deut 5:16) and to keep one's sacred vows (Ps 76:11). The Talmud contains commentary showing that this issue had been considered and that at least some rabbis argued for a path by which someone could repent of a vow if it ended up conflicting with a higher obligation. There was also a specific rabbinic tradition applying this to obligations to parents.[2]

Probably this legal argument was ongoing during Jesus' time and had not been resolved. Perhaps Jesus, activated as he always was by justice and compassion, was outraged at examples of needy parents being left out in the cold because of vows that should never have been made by their thoughtless grown children. Convincing people to sacrifice their parents' well-being to enrich the temple coffers would have been guaranteed to make Jesus mad. One can think of more than a few modern parallels, like TV evangelists seducing people to give their last dollar to help buy these preachers nice airplanes. As Emerson Powery puts it, "Economic care for the elderly is more fundamental than 'tithes' for religious institutions!"[3]

Any ethicist will notice that this issue of a conflict between two or more positive moral obligations is a classic one in our field. A great example is the potential conflict between the obligation to save a life and the obligation to tell the truth. What if you are hiding Jews in your attic and Nazis are at the door demanding to know if you have any Jews around? If you tell

---

2. Wills, in JANT, 84.

3. Powery, "Gospel of Mark," in Blount, *True to Our Native Land*, 134. Exclamation mark in the original. It should be noted that Jesus' movement could also have been accused of encouraging followers to abandon their obligations to their families as they left them behind to follow him.

the truth, you sacrifice life. If you do not tell the truth, you save life, but at the cost of truth.

This situation was often faced during the Holocaust. Most everyone intuited that saving life was a weightier obligation than telling the truth. We have this concept in ethics called *prima facie* moral norms—on first appearance, or on its face, one has a specific obligation, like telling the truth. But in real life, a *prima facie* obligation like that might be overridden by a higher obligation, like saving life. This is a common facet of everyday ethics.

To get back to our case in this text, if someone understood the obligation to keep a sacred vow to God to be weightier than the obligation to support their needy parents, that would seem to most of us a failure of moral discernment, a bad judgment call. And yet extreme vow-keeping was not unprecedented in Scripture—consider the awful story of Jephthah (Judg 11) killing his daughter because of his foolish vow to sacrifice the first thing he saw when he walked through his door after the miraculous defeat of the Ammonites. The first thing he saw was his daughter. But he did it anyway.

The debate over tradition then moves to the Pharisees' interpretation of ritual purity in the preparation and eating of food (Matt 7:14–21). It has been a common Christian interpretation of this passage to suggest that Jesus abrogated Jewish dietary regulations altogether. However, Jewish Talmudic scholar Daniel Boyarin argues persuasively that what Jesus actually does is argue with a relatively recent Pharisaic innovation related to ritual hand washing before eating. They taught that failure to follow proper ritual hand washing procedure could render the food touched by the hands unclean, and thus render the eater ritually impure. It is this innovation that Jesus is rejecting. The issue, then, was not Jewish food laws per se, but recent Pharisaic ritual purity innovations.

Still, the concluding point comes with thunderous power: *from within, from the human heart* (Mark 7:21) is where the real defilement emerges. Evil actions and attitudes come from within, and they are more important than whether I eat pork or wash my hands in a specific way. Food and purity laws (or any other list of publicly observable obligations) can easily be understood not to get to the heart of morality. One can think of many people who are very good at obeying religious rules but many of whose actions are simply wretched. Jesus says, give me a pure heart and deeds of mercy rather than ritual purity, if a choice must be made. This was already a major theme in the prophets (cf. Hos 6:6).

The damaging potential of this passage in terms of Jewish-Christian relations is actualized when Christians posit themselves as the inwardly good, clean-hearted, law-free types, with Jews (exemplified by the Pharisees) as the inwardly evil, dark-hearted legalists. Such pridefulness via comparison has often afflicted us and hurt those with whom we have compared ourselves. Typical lines in Christian Bible commentaries often reinforce this tendency, to wit: "Jesus turns their niggling complaint about his disciples' conduct into a caustic condemnation of their whole tradition . . . Jesus insists . . . that they have drifted away from God, who cares nothing about their ablutions or their lip service."[4]

Not to belabor the point, but again we say that an enduring moral issue is what, if any, binding, lawlike moral obligations we end up with in Christianity. Catholics, for example, have holy days of obligation and a periodic requirement to go to Confession. These are the rules. Period. Why? Because the Church says this is how we honor God. That doesn't mean all Catholics obey the rules, but there are rules, and Catholics *do know what the rules are.*

Nonfundamentalist Protestants tend to avoid such an understanding of lawlike moral obligations, preferring to focus on the inner life and motivations of the believer. Biblical scholar James Edwards offers a common Christian trope when he says the lesson of this passage is that "the foundation of morality is a matter of inward purity, motive, and intent rather than of external compliance to ritual and custom."[5]

But is there no role for binding obligations that go beyond the state of the human heart and the most important moral deeds and misdeeds? Perhaps we would do better to move in a both/and rather than either/or direction here. We need to know that some actions are simply mandatory, while others are simply forbidden. Adultery, for example, is an act, and it is forbidden for Christians (Matt 5:27–30, 19:9, 19:18). Giving alms to the poor is an act, and it is mandatory for Christians (Matt 6:2, Luke 12:33). Still, we also need to know that underlying all actions is the human heart, whose true state, while reflected in our actions, is ultimately known only to God.

4. Garland, *Mark*, 271, 273.
5. Edwards, *Mark*, 214.

5

Deny Yourself

*If any wish to come after me, let them deny themselves and take up
their cross and follow me. For those who want to save their life will
lose it, and those who lose their life for my sake, and for the gospel,
will save it. For what will it profit them to gain the whole world and
forfeit their life?*

—*MARK 8:34–36*

Texts: Mark 8:27—9:1/Matt 16:13–28/Luke 9:18–27

THIS PASSAGE BEGINS WITH Jesus asking his disciples how the people are
thinking about him—what is his identity, what is God doing through him
and with him? Various answers are offered, all of them prophetic figures.
Then Jesus asks them what they think. Peter comes through with the decisive affirmation: Jesus is the Messiah.

The concept of Messiah (Hebrew: *mashiach*, Greek: *christos*) meant
"anointed one." It had been applied to Jewish kings, high priests, and prophets. By the time of Jesus, it had been taken by many to mean the promised
future God-anointed king in the line of David, the disrupted Israelite royal
dynasty (Ps 89:19–37). This figure could be projected to be human or supernatural or both, with a regular lifetime or an eternal one. His role would

be to redeem Israel, throw off her enemies, reclaim the Holy Land, and restore right relations between God and Israel (cf. Luke 1:46–79). For some, this was what the concept of the kingdom of God, or at least its inauguration, was taken to mean.[1] Messianic hope had intensified in the period just before Jesus emerged, reflecting deep political frustrations among the Jewish people.[2]

Considering the mixed background of the term's use in the Hebrew Bible, and the great political and spiritual stress under which the Jewish people were living, it is perhaps not surprising that first-century Jews both had messianic hopes but also a variety of visions as to what exactly the Messiah would be and would do. It certainly seems clear that when Peter first articulated the idea that Jesus was Israel's Messiah, which Jesus privately affirmed with them, they were expecting a figure who would come in triumph, not one who would "undergo great suffering, and be rejected . . . and be killed, and after three days rise again" (Mark 8:31). We will see several passages later in the narrative of Jesus in which, despite what Jesus says here, his disciples are still anticipating earthly triumph and rule—both for Jesus and themselves.

Think of Christianity as containing within itself multiple great mysteries, such as how a person could do the miracles Jesus did, or how someone could rise from the dead. I would suggest that from a Jewish perspective, the first great mystery, a nearly insuperable one, is how a genuine Messiah could be crucified (cf. Luke 24:13–35). The fact that Jesus has this exchange with his disciples on the way to Caesarea Philippi (Mark 8:27) should not be missed. In Jesus' time it was largely non-Jewish in population and had become a site of Roman and Herodian power and pagan worship.[3] This is the kind of place that a revolutionary-political type of Messiah would be expected to overthrow. But instead, it is where Jesus announces that he is the kind of Messiah who will be murdered by the authorities.

Peter cannot imagine this kind of Messiah, and so he rebukes his Lord. Jesus fires back at him with the most explosive rebuke that we ever see him offer to any disciple in the Gospels: "Get behind me, Satan!" (Mark 8:33). He then calls the crowd and the disciples together and offers this crucial teaching about discipleship: it involves self-denial, cross-bearing, and following after; it involves self-abandonment for Jesus and the gospel,

1. Powery, "Gospel of Mark," in Blount, *True to Our Native Land*, 138.

2. Edwards, *Mark*, 250.

3. Edwards, *Mark*, 246; Garland, *Mark*, 323.

a dying to self that is the path to true life. He makes clear that the rejection and suffering he will undergo, they will share, "in this adulterous and sinful generation" (Mark 8:38). Their suffering and dishonor, alongside his, will both give evidence of the sinful rebelliousness of the world and will also hasten its judgment. But in their fidelity to Jesus, they will be spared the coming judgment (Mark 8:38—9:1).

This passage, then, at one level is tightly tied to the specifics of the first-century events around the life and death of Jesus. Jesus was preparing his disciples, and those who would wish to be his disciples, for his and their rejection, persecution, suffering, and death. He was warning them that this was the path he was taking and that if they wanted to follow him it was the path that they would be taking as well. And, of course, he was right— in the initial Jesus movement, periodically in the first three centuries of Christianity, and in some places even today, this is exactly what being a Christ-follower has entailed: a bearing of the cross for the sake of Jesus and his kingdom of justice and righteousness.[4]

This does not exhaust the meaning of the teaching, however. It has a broader resonance, or at least has been interpreted as such: that *the pattern of a Christian's life is to be cruciform*—cross-shaped. Genuine Christian commitment is to a life of self-denial, cross-bearing, and following-after. "He does not ask disciples to deny something to themselves but to deny the self and all self-promoting ambitions . . . Those who deny themselves have learned to say, 'Not my will but thine be done.'"[5]

This teaching has had a complex legacy. On the one hand, it has inspired a great many earnest Christ-followers into lives of selfless and sometimes risky service, abandoning self-interest while following Jesus. As Dietrich Bonhoeffer wrote, "Self-denial means knowing only Christ, no longer knowing oneself. It means no longer seeing oneself, only him who is going ahead, no longer seeing the way which is too difficult for us. Self-denial says only: he is going ahead, hold fast to him."[6]

I think of one of my heroes, Florence Nightingale, who held to an unorthodox theology but who was completely invested in this vision of a self-sacrificing life of service to others. She embodied this while working twenty-hour days to save the lives of soldiers who were dying in the Crimean

---

4. Powery, "Gospel of Mark," in Blount, *True to Our Native Land*, 138.

5. Garland, *Mark*, 327.

6. Bonhoeffer, *Discipleship*, 86.

War from insanely bad medical facilities.[7] I also think of Bonhoeffer himself, who saw the life-imperiling path ahead of him and his companions when they chose anti-Nazi resistance—and then went ahead and paid that price anyway. Service and the risk of death, all just being part of the deal you sign up for when you sign up for Jesus—this has been a powerful dimension of some of the most morally productive lives in Christian history.

On the other hand, the downside of this teaching, at least for some, has been as a counsel of permanent subordination—unevenly visited on those without power. How many women, for example, have historically been told to deny themselves and their needs in order to serve their husbands? How many times has "suffering for the sake of suffering" been inculcated precisely onto the weary shoulders of those who are mistreated in this world?[8] The moral norm to be embraced is not the suffering, *but the obedient following-after Jesus*, which has the *potential* for bringing suffering our way.

This is a teaching especially valuable for extreme situations in which persecution and suffering may become our lot as Christians. All who are considering Christian commitment should be reminded, as Bonhoeffer said into the teeth of the Nazi regime, "When Christ calls a [person], he bids him come and die."[9] It is also a teaching more broadly about a life of service. It speaks to the "following-after" dimension of Christian discipleship. We go where he leads.

Bonhoeffer understood that Christ's call offers us a choice to follow. "No one can be forced, no one can even be expected to follow him . . . everything depends on decision."[10] Such decisions can only be made by free people, not subjugated ones. The good news is that when we follow him wherever he leads, even into suffering and sacrifice, by doing so we actually find the truest, highest meaning of our lives.

---

7. See Gushee and Holtz, *Moral Leadership for a Divided Age*, ch. 3.

8. Emerson Powery, "Gospel of Mark," in Blount, *True to Our Native Land*, 138.

9. Bonhoeffer, *Discipleship*, original English translation, 87.

10. Bonhoeffer, *Discipleship*, 86.

6

True Greatness

Whoever wants to be first must be last of all and servant of all.

—MARK 9:35

For the Son of Man came not to be served but to serve, and to give his life a ransom for many.

—MARK 10:45

Texts: Mark 9:33–37/Matt 18:1–5/Luke 9:46–48, Mark 10:35–45/Matt 20:20–28/Luke 22:24–27

TWO DIFFERENT EVENTS, EACH with parallel versions in the Synoptic Gospels, give embarrassing accounts of the disciples' all-too-human quest for recognition as the greatest of the Twelve. In Mark 9/Matt 18/Luke 9, the first event is set in Galilee, before the decisive trek to Jerusalem and the cross. In Mark 10/Matt 20/Luke 22, the second event is set on that final journey.

I think these moral teachings Jesus offers belong together, so that is how we are studying them here. Both teach essentially the same thing: don't do what comes naturally; don't grasp for power and status; true greatness is found in service and self-sacrifice. But the fact that the cross is looming makes the second event, the story of the grasping James and John (and their mother!), even more striking. And something important is going on here in relation to the moral status of children.

In Mark's version of the first incident (Mark 9:33–37), the disciples are with Jesus in his home base of Capernaum. He has overheard an argument among them over who is the greatest. When he asks them about it, they are shamed into silence. After all, this conversation was taking place just after Jesus' prediction of his own death (Mark 9:30–32). Perhaps they were sorting out who would be his earthly successor! He's not even dead yet and they are fighting over his position.

Jesus then sits the Twelve down for an important talk.[1] In this talk he articulates the key principle that being truly "first" means making oneself "last." Being truly great means taking up servanthood (Mark 9:35). Then he holds a little child and says that welcoming a child in Jesus' name is welcoming him and the one who sent him (Mark 9:36–37). This is to identify himself and God with children—the very littlest and least significant. It also reminds us of Matt 25:31–46, where Jesus identifies himself with the hungry, the thirsty, and the stranger, with the naked, sick, and imprisoned (see ch. 40 below). It is really important how often Jesus, in both word and action, identifies with the marginalized, with those in need of succor and support.

Matthew's version of this event (Matt 18:1–5) has a few interesting changes. Here it is the disciples asking, "who is the greatest in the kingdom of heaven?" (Matt 18:1), as opposed to asking which one of us is the next great man. (Is it any wonder that the Greek word for "greatest" here, *megas*, can also be rendered as arrogant?) Jesus again brings a child forward to answer their somewhat more innocent question—true greatness involves the need to change and become like children, and the need to be humble like a child. And then finally comes the saying about welcoming the child amounting to welcoming Jesus.

Don't miss the way Jesus teaches the lessons to be learned from close engagement with children. We must "receive" what children have to teach us. But what exactly does Jesus want us to see when we look at children?

David Garland emphasizes the "insignificance of the child on the honor scale. The child had no power, no status, and few rights."[2] The teaching is that disciples should voluntarily descend the honor scale, to go where children already dwell, and then from that position to serve the humble in

---

1. Edwards, *Mark*, 286, emphasizes the unique move Jesus makes with the Twelve here, to sit them down for an authoritative teaching on the spot.

2. Garland, *Mark*, 367.

all humility.[3] For Garland, Jesus is using children as an illustration rather than focusing on children themselves.[4]

In my view, Jesus wants to teach us to value all people, especially those of little power or status in our cultures—including the deeply vulnerable human child, who does receive Jesus' specific attention, and not only in this passage. *Children are not just an object lesson for Jesus*—they are moral subjects, worthy of value.

But I also believe Jesus wants us to receive from children a particular moral lesson that is not related to their cultural marginality, but instead to their typical approach to the world. We can notice that little children, especially, have not yet learned to seek status the way that the much less wise grown-ups around them so feverishly do. That toxic formation in status-seeking and honor culture is still ahead of them. Better if they never learn it. Better if we adults unlearn status-seeking by learning from our own children.[5]

I think that this is what Jesus is teaching us to receive from attending to the lives of children.

The second event (Mark 10:35–45) is probably a bit more familiar to most readers. James and John (or their mother, in Matthew), on the very road to the cross, pull Jesus aside and ask for the top places when Jesus comes into his kingdom. Jesus states that they will indeed partake of the "cup" and the "baptism" (of suffering, of blood) that he will endure (Mark 10:38). But their place-seeking is entirely out of place. And the disciples' indignation (Mark 10:41) is not much better, because it seems more competitive than morally outraged.

But abandoning status-seeking is what Jesus demands. It is the entire model of earthly power and status-seeking that must be renounced. He makes a comparison to gentile paradigms of rule: in Mark, that is "lording it over" and "tyranny"; in Luke, it is being a "benefactor," patron, the master at the feast. For Jesus, true greatness, again, takes the form of servanthood.

---

3. Garland, *Mark*, 367.

4. Edwards, *Mark*, 288, also views the reference to children as an example of insignificance, not as really being about children themselves.

5. Both Garland and Edwards warn against any romanticized or sentimentalized modern reading of Jesus' reference to children, which would be anachronistic in relation to the attitudes and practices of the first-century world (Garland, *Mark*, 367; Edwards, *Mark*, 288). Yes, but—it seems to me that Jesus is valuing children themselves, not just as examples, and that Jesus cares about their well-being.

It is interesting that Luke situates this conversation during the Last Supper (Luke 22:24–27). His is the only Gospel to do that. This heightens the drama of the story considerably and may account for what Luke does next. In his version, Luke has Jesus spell out something at this moment that Mark and Matthew only have Jesus imply—that there will one day be an eschatological "table" in a "kingdom," and "thrones" on which these disciples (Luke 22:29–30), who "have stood by me in my trials" (Luke 22:28) will sit. But this is *on the other side* of the cross, in the messianic age, at the time of the "renewal of all things" (Matt 19:28). It is not now. Now is the time for service, suffering, and sacrifice. Jesus is about to demonstrate bodily the only path to that messianic banquet—the cross.

These passages can be understood to teach something that might seem familiar if one is a long-time member of a Christian church—if we want to be great, we should look to serve humbly. While human beings may not honor us, God is watching, and God's verdict is the one that matters. This teaching, repeated in two places and demonstrated by Jesus himself, is a powerful if plaintive call for his followers to be different from everyday worldlings who spend so much of their lives jockeying for title, status, and position. (Which one of us gets to be assistant regional manager at Dunder-Mifflin in Scranton? We're going to have to fight it out!) What a waste of emotion, intention, and effort all this jockeying for position turns out to be, this scramble for power, this knifing (sometimes literally) to be one up on the next person.

But if we read Jesus a bit more eschatologically, the teaching takes on a different flavor. The desire for God's kingdom and a place at the head table is not so much denounced but transfigured—that table exists, that kingdom is coming, and we might just get a place at it. But only if we follow Jesus on that path of service, selflessness, and sacrifice that ended for him on a Roman cross.

7

Temptation

"If any of you cause one of these little ones who believe in me[1] *to sin, it would be better for you if a great millstone were hung around your neck and you were thrown into the sea."*

—MARK 9:42

"If your hand or your foot causes you to sin, cut it off and throw it away; it is better for you to enter life maimed or lame than to have two hands or two feet and to be thrown into the eternal fire."

—MATT 18:8

Texts: Mark 9:42–48/Matt 18:6–9, cf. Luke 17:1–2

THIS STERN PASSAGE CONCERNS the temptation to sin. Two memorable sayings of Jesus are combined in the versions offered by Matthew and Mark, offering two different but related lessons about the seriousness of sin and the requirement for disciples to resist temptation.

In Matthew and Mark, the reference to "little ones" (*mikron*) comes in near proximity to the scene where Jesus presents a child to the disciples

---

1. NT manuscripts differ as to the inclusion of "in me" in this passage.

(Matt 18:1–5, Mark 9:33–37). As we saw in the last chapter, the exact lesson to be drawn from Jesus' discussion of children is not agreed, but it was clear that Jesus had children around him, celebrated something special about their character, identified with them, and called for disciples to welcome them. Mark's version is especially striking because Jesus takes the child in his arms (Mark 9:36).

In this passage, Jesus' stern words of warning about causing one of these little ones who believe (in him) to sin, or to "stumble" (NRSV; Gk: *skandalon*) should be read in light of the presence of little children in the immediately preceding context.[2] While the warning has wider potential application, it seems to me that Jesus is making a statement that is specifically about causing moral harm to children. This Greek word, *skandalon*, could also be translated as anyone who "sets a trap for." When one thinks of the specific vulnerability of children, the traps that unscrupulous adults sometimes set for children, the harm so often done to children, it ought to cause all of us to shudder.

Jesus' warning is that anyone, certainly any purported disciple, who "scandalizes" a child, anyone who leads a child to sin, anyone who destroys the innocence of a child, has committed a grave sin for which divine punishment is fully appropriate. Think, for example, of the various church contexts that we now know about in which the sexual abuse of children and teens has been permitted and covered up. Children have been harmed, and their faith shattered, in the very houses of God where they were supposed to be most safe.

We must not become tempters in relation to children. The warning appears to be directed within the Christ-following community due to its reference to children who believe in Jesus. We must not be the ones who cause immature young believers to lose their way, to stumble, to fall into a trap, to sin.

Only in Matthew do we have these words: "Woe to the world because of things that cause sin! Such things are bound to come, but woe to the one through whom they come!" (Matt 18:7)

Jesus here acknowledges that in this broken world, this world in rebellion against its one true King, various occasions and temptations to sin arise. They are "bound to come"—though they are to be strenuously resisted. The

---

2. This claim contradicts Edwards, *Mark*, 292, who says it is about causing believers to sin. But this misses the immediate context and once again obscures the place of children in Jesus' moral vision.

warning here is not to be the ones through whom these temptations come. We need to care deeply about the moral well-being of those who are affected by us, especially "little ones," e.g., children and young people, or—in a reasonable extension—those who are less mature in the journey of faith.

This teaching has had a big impact and a long career in Christian church life. It has been widely used in evangelical and fundamentalist circles to warn believers against being a "stumbling block" to others—I think especially of young women being warned repeatedly to dress modestly so as not to tempt the lustful eyes of their male friends.

This exemplifies a problematic potential interpretation of this teaching: Person A's sinful choice can be wrongly attributed to Person B, whereas each of us should instead be taught to take responsibility for our own choices. For example, in the Sermon on the Mount, when Jesus teaches about sexual lust (Matt 5:27–30) he places full responsibility on the one desiring, not the one desired. Perhaps we can now see that this passage has been badly misapplied in some Christian contexts in relation to the issue of sexuality, treating the lustful male as if he is a little one unable to discipline his own desires.

In each version of the "stumbling block" teaching in the Synoptic Gospels, it is "little ones" who are in view, not peers. This makes sense. In relation to children and young people, adults have a special responsibility of solicitude and care. It is wrong to expose the young to things they are not ready to encounter. It is beyond wrong—pure evil—to intentionally destroy the innocence of a child, as through sexual grooming and abuse.

It is worth noting that the Greek term *mikros*, being translated to "little ones," can mean "little" in almost any sense of the word, such as small of age, stature, status, faith, intellect, education, finances, capabilities, etc. The image of the child is expanded to include the vulnerable in all times and places.

As a teacher and pastor, I have long believed it is appropriate to extend the implication of this teaching to my own vocation. It is indeed the responsibility of Christian leaders not to place stumbling blocks, or occasions of temptation, before those in our charge. We must carefully consider what we teach, how we teach, and how we treat those under our care. This vocational responsibility connects to striking passages like this one in James: "Not many of you should become teachers, my brothers and sisters, for you know that we who teach will face stricter judgment" (Jas 3:1).

Let us move on to the second half of this pericope as recorded in Matthew and in Mark. That is the metaphoric-hyperbolic teaching[3] that it would be better to destroy one's own tempting hand, foot, or eye than to go to hell with the full original set. This is potentially problematic, but there is a teaching of great value here. It has to do with the seriousness of effort we should be willing to undertake to avoid falling into temptation. As James Edwards puts it, "The metaphors of eyes, hands, and feet are all-inclusive of what we view, what we do, where we go."[4] They are not only about sexual sins.

A point to remember is that it is not actually the eye, foot, or hand that "causes" sin. It is the will and desire of the person whose body includes eyes, feet, and hands. Certainly, Jesus' teaching here must be read as hyperbole, or metaphor, as a picturesque way of describing sinful desires and actions. If I use my eyes, hands, and feet to steal your car, it is not my limbs that are responsible. It is my misdirected and undisciplined coveting of your vehicle.

Jesus is teaching followers to make every effort to practice God's will rather than disobey it. We cannot be casual about sinning against God. A variety of forces in the contemporary church have contributed to diminishing our focus on temptation and the effort to resist it. Not wanting to be old-fashioned, judgmental, or legalistic, we no longer teach or speak much about temptation, sin, and the moral struggle within the Christian soul to choose the way of obedience. Perhaps this helps account for the moral sloppiness of the contemporary Christian scene.

For those who might still be reluctant to speak about temptation, it might help to remember that for Jesus it is most often sins against neighbor, against the poor, against children (as in this case), against widows, against the outcast, against the vulnerable, that attract his greatest attention. In offering warnings against temptations to sin against the weak, Jesus stands firmly in the prophetic tradition. There is no reason for us to shy away from following him in that emphasis and imposing the moral demands on ourselves that he is already making of us in these texts.

The teaching that God is watching how we live, how we treat one another, especially those most vulnerable, is worthy of emphasis in our cruel and morally indifferent age. We are rightly warned against giving in to the temptation to sin against God and our neighbors, especially those most vulnerable to the harm we can do to them.

3. See Edwards, *Mark*, 293, for that description.
4. Edwards, *Mark*, 294.

8

Marriage, Divorce, and Children

"They are no longer two, but one flesh. Therefore what God has joined together, let no one separate."

—MARK 10:8B–9

Texts: Mark 10:1–16/Matt 19:1–15/Luke 16:18, cf. Luke 18:15–17

JESUS' RIGOROUS TEACHING ON divorce clearly gave the early church great difficulties. One sign of the difficulties is the editing undertaken by Matthew of Mark's version, an edit that treated Jesus' teaching as church law but added a loophole allowing divorce for *porneia*—probably sexual misconduct, but the interpretation is debated. The term *porneia* appears twenty-six times in the New Testament. If Jesus meant to say "adultery," the Greek word *moicheia* would have been the more appropriate choice.

Another sign of the early church's struggle is that Paul both reports Jesus' teaching in 1 Cor 7:10–11 and feels the need to offer some improvised case law to go with it (1 Cor 7:12–16). For centuries the church has continued to wrestle with what Jesus said about divorce; consensus disappeared centuries ago. These days, in almost every part of the church it has been modified, adapted, or set aside, at least in practice.

I have offered extensive analysis of these texts in three other books.[1] I will be brief here. In Mark's version, Jesus is asked by some Pharisees, who are trying to trap him, whether it is lawful for a man to divorce his wife.[2] Jesus asks what Moses commanded. The Pharisees allude to Deut 24:1–4, which spells out the process in Torah by which a man could write a certificate of divorce and send his wife away. Jesus says this was a concession to their "hardness of heart" (Mark 10:5), and trumps this legal text with the creation account (Gen 2:18–25), stressing the divine origins of marriage and the one-flesh (Gen 1:27, 2:24) nature of the relationship.

The most straightforward reading of Jesus' teaching in Mark 10:9 is that Jesus simply bans divorce. When the disciples ask him about this privately, he declares divorce followed by remarriage to be equivalent to adultery (Mark 10:10–12). Both Mark and Matthew place the story of Jesus blessing and honoring children as the next event in his ministry. Luke places it separately (Luke 18:15–17) but retains a version of the teaching against remarriage (Luke 16:18).

Several contextual notes are relevant here. One is that the rigorist, eschatological Qumran sect, contemporaneous with Jesus, also entirely prohibited divorce based on marriage being ordained in creation.[3] Also, OT law explains a process by which men could initiate divorce; women's right to divorce is not mentioned. Roman law (under which the Jewish people lived) contradicted this by also permitting women to initiate divorce, though this apparently was very rare and mainly among the upper classes. Mark's version reflects this possibility of women initiating divorce, but Matthew's does not, which may reflect differences in the contexts in which they were writing. Elizabeth Malbon, in *The Women's Bible Commentary*, suggests that Mark's language about women's ability to initiate divorce is an intentional choice by the author to demonstrate Jesus' radical inclusivity toward women.[4]

1. Gushee, *Getting Marriage Right*; Gushee, *Introducing Christian Ethics*, ch. 19; Gushee/Stassen, *Kingdom Ethics*, ch. 14.

2. Garland, *Mark*, 378, points out the political vulnerability of Jesus in relation to this question. John the Baptist had been thrown in jail and finally executed for challenging King Herod's divorce and then remarriage to his brother's wife (Mark 6:17–29). This kind of spouse-shopping and -swapping was common among the Romans but scandalous to devout Jews.

3. Wills, in JANT, 91.

4. Malbon, "Gospel of Mark," in *Women's Bible Commentary*, 487. Edwards, *Mark*, 304–5, finds evidence that Jewish women were permitted to divorce their husbands in

Some of Jesus' disciples were separating from their spouses to follow Jesus, and possibly embracing what we might call a permanent posture of end-times celibacy. This was a definite breach with Jewish tradition and with Paul's later prohibition on withholding sex from one's spouse under the heightened passion of eschatological fervor (1 Cor 7:3–5). Though it is debated, this question may be what Jesus refers to in the discussion in Matt 19:10–12 about eunuchs for the kingdom.[5]

The strictness of the grounds for divorce was a matter of rabbinic discussion around the time of Jesus and is reflected in Talmudic references to a debate between the schools of Hillel and Shammai. The issue was whether divorce could be for any reason or only for a serious reason, perhaps associated with sexual transgression. The looser view was permitting divorce for the most trivial of reasons, including mere preference for another woman.[6] This was being justified through a creative (that is, destructive) reading of Deut 24:1.

It is also relevant to remember that life expectancy was much shorter in Jesus' time, that there was no birth control, and that many women died in childbirth. Women often did not have full agency regarding who they were to marry, and cultural expectations of interpersonal intimacy and loving relationship are a feature far more of our culture than of the ancient world.

This profound cultural gap between our world and the world of the text must be kept in mind as we read this teaching. People in the advanced world today generally live to be about eighty, have agency over whether or whom they marry, have access to birth control, do not necessarily marry with the hope of having children, tend to have high interpersonal-relational expectations, have full legal access to divorce for any and every reason—and this is all true of women as well as men.

Christians, as well, rarely live with the heightened sense of an imminent end of history that would leave them willing to endure the short-term sacrifice of an unhappy marriage or sexless life. Remember how Paul suggests that since Jesus will be back soon (1 Cor 7:25–31), Christians should abstain from marriage unless they burn with passion (1 Cor 7:36) and simply must get married. It is possible that Jesus himself also taught about marriage with a very short time horizon in mind, as did the Qumran

Judaism, and not just under Roman law, during this time period.

5. JANT, 46.

6. JANT, 46; cf. Gushee/Stassen, *Kingdom Ethics*, 277–78; Edwards, *Mark*, 299–300.

community. But it is also possible that such a shortened time horizon had little to do with Jesus' teaching against divorce.

Jesus' ban or near ban on divorce does not land well with many modern people, even serious Christians. It asks more than most Christians are willing to endure—not just if their spouses have committed some obvious "cause" for divorce, like adultery, but also if the marriage is a relational hellscape. This is why most church traditions, pastors, and Christians have in one way or another set aside this ban on divorce. This matter was debated intensely decades ago, but that debate is long forgotten in most churches.

I do want to suggest another possible angle of vision. If we assume a Jewish audience for Jesus' original teaching, with a starting point being a biblical text (Deut 24:1–4) that assumes only men could initiate a divorce, and a rabbinic debate over the legitimate grounds for divorce, Jesus is probably best read as taking Shammai's position—divorce only on the grounds of adultery, or sexual misconduct of some sort. This position on Jesus' part would reflect his respect for God's intentions for marriage, his profound concern for women's and children's well-being, and his overall commitment to social justice for those most vulnerable to injustice.

Is it too much to imagine Jesus saying to his male audience: how dare you misread both the letter and the spirit of God's law to abandon your wives and throw your children into misery? That is just adultery, it violates the seventh commandment, and it certainly violates God's intent for marriage.

What that says about our divorce situations today—many of which are about interpersonal misery, not mere preference for someone new—is not an easy question.

One other thing. What does it mean to say that marriage is a "one-flesh" relationship (Gen 2:24, Mark 10:8)? We tend to think of sexual intercourse, and of romantic and interpersonal unity.[7] But children should also be seen as the literal one-flesh embodiment of marital love. Especially in a no-birth-control context such as Jesus' own, surely people would have thought about children and marriage in a close, intertwining way. The "two become one flesh" when they have sex, and through their act they create one flesh—a new human being who lives because of the relationship between her parents. A child who is a literal embodiment of her parents' oneness.

---

7. Powery, "Gospel of Mark," in Blount, *True to Our Native Land*, 140, emphasizes the gender egalitarianism of the concept: "At the heart of Jesus' teaching is a statement of equality."

Whatever happens to the relationship between the parents who co-created with God to bring a new life into the world, that couple's children will always be their one-flesh embodiment. It has indeed been so "since creation." Jesus' teachings on divorce and children go together. I think he is reminding those who would casually divorce that there is much more at stake than their personal happiness.

9

A Rich Man Seeks Salvation

Then Jesus looked around and said to his disciples, "How hard it will be for those who have wealth to enter the kingdom of God!"

—MARK 10:23

Texts: Mark 10:17–31/Matt 19:16–30/Luke 18:18–30

IT ALMOST ALWAYS BRINGS significant insight when we study closely both the similarities and the differences between different Gospel accounts of the same event. This story, often called the "rich young ruler," though only in Luke is he a ruler, and nowhere is he identified as young, contains more similarities than differences in the three Gospel accounts. However, there are a few interesting differences. Let's walk through the nine movements of this story.

1. *The questioner's mode of address.* In Mark, the man runs up, kneels before Jesus, and addresses him as "Good Teacher." The mood is respectful, even supplicatory. In Matthew and in Luke, the greetings feel more peer-to-peer. A man walks up to Jesus and asks a question—though in Luke the greeting is also "Good Teacher."

2. *The question itself.* Matthew differs from Mark and Luke in having the rich man ask the question this way: "What good deed must I do to inherit eternal life?" The commentator in the notes to the *Jewish*

Annotated New Testament claims flatly that the man's question is illegitimate within the framework of covenantal Judaism.[1] Thus, it should not be a question of an individual Jew accruing merit points based on specific deeds. Still, in all three Gospels, the seriousness of the man's question seems real enough to him—this is a person who genuinely wants to know what is required for him to enter eternal life. We should take his question seriously on its own terms.

3. *Jesus' initial rebuff.* In each version, Jesus pushes back against the use of the word "good" (Gk: *agathos*) in the opening question. In Mark and Luke: "Why do you call me good? No one is good but God alone." In all versions, Jesus rebuffs the ascription of goodness to himself, and directs attention to the goodness of God (Mark 10:18/Matt 19:17/ Luke 18:19). It is not clear why this move is important to him. Perhaps he is veiling his messianic/divine identity for the time being.[2] Perhaps he finds the greeting to be "idle flattery."[3]

4. *Jesus' answer is "keep the commandments."* In Mark and Luke, Jesus moves on to tell the man that the latter knows the commandments, and then goes on enumerate six commandments—the human interpersonal ones, the moral ones, essentially the "second table of the Law."[4] It is as if Jesus is saying, "Why are you asking me this question? You know the Law, do that." What does it say about the way Jesus thought about God's will that when asked about entering eternal life he focuses exclusively on the second table of the Law—on violence, covenant breaking in marriage, theft, bearing false witness, fraud, and honoring parents? It says that Jesus cared deeply about morality in human relations, as many of his contemporaries did.

5. *Questioner response.* In all three versions, the questioner affirms that he has obeyed these commands. He has not violated even one of them "since my youth." In no version of the Gospels does Jesus challenge the accuracy of this answer. That is interesting, because a certain kind of introspective, overscrupulous version of Christian ethics would suggest that human sin is so pervasive that *no one could ever keep all these*

---

1. JANT, 46.

2. Edwards, *Mark*, 310.

3. Garland, *Mark*, 395.

4. Edwards, *Mark*, 310, notes Jesus' substitution of "do not defraud" for the ban on coveting. Matt 19:19 adds "love your neighbor as yourself."

commands. Jesus does not make that kind of move here, accepting that it is possible that this young man has never murdered, stolen, defrauded, and so on.

6. *What he still lacks.* All three Gospel accounts agree that this man still lacks something. The issue is most poignant in Matthew's version, where the man himself senses the lack. In Mark and Luke, Jesus intuits that something more is needed here. Mark alone has the memorable line: "Jesus, looking at him, loved him."[5] It is as if in Matthew, the man realizes a spiritual need, whereas in Mark and Luke, Jesus sees it and names it. The prescription is the same in each of the three accounts: go home, sell all you have and give the proceeds to the poor, come and follow me, now as a possessor only of treasure in heaven. Only in Matthew does Jesus frame his answer this way: "If you wish to be perfect," go . . . etc. This move helped to create a tradition, most explicit in Catholicism and Orthodoxy, in which economic divestment was required of those seeking the highest spiritual path, such as those taking religious orders (monks and nuns), but not of others. This is one highly practical way to interpret and apply, but ultimately soften the power of this story for most Christians.

7. *The man's response.* The inquirer senses that he has a spiritual need that goes beyond obeying these commandments. Jesus responds by giving him a harder challenge—total economic divestment and life on the road with himself. Only now does the reader learn the man is wealthy. Only now do we see the one thing he is not willing to do to inherit eternal life—he is not willing to give up his rather abundant possessions. Having said no to his one path to the life he longs for, the man walks away sadly.

8. *Explicit follow-up teaching by Jesus.* The man is gone but Jesus is not done teaching. He says to his disciples and anyone else within earshot—"How hard it will be for those who have wealth to enter the kingdom of God!" (Mark 10:23). He was calling the man to sell, and give, and leave his entire hometown life behind. And this he was unwilling to do.[6]

5. Powery, "Gospel of Mark," in Blount, *True to Our Native Land,* 141, points out that "this is the *only time* in Mark that the author describes Jesus' love for anyone." Jesus must have been quite moved by the man's urgent spiritual search.

6. Wills, in JANT, 91, points out the radicalism of Jesus' teaching to this man and that the rabbis explicitly disavowed total divestment because it would put one's family at risk.

9. *Encouragement for those who have taken the plunge.* Peter articulates the heart's cry of the whole itinerant band as he says, Look, Jesus, we have left our "homes" (Luke only), we have left "everything" (Mark, Matthew) to follow you. Whatever else one may say about the Twelve, this was true; they did this radical thing, and Jesus closes the passage by affirming them for it, and promising abundant rewards both now and in the age to come. Mark (10:31) and Matthew (19:30) end by appending this memorable saying: "Many who are first will be last, and the last will be first." When placed here, this seems to mean: the rich folks of this world, the ones in first place who keep living their lives and enjoying their wealth and sacrificing nothing, will end up last in God's kingdom; but those who have left all, and will suffer much, will end up first.

This text has always inspired and troubled the church that has taken it seriously. It was broadly understood as a counsel of radical economic divestment in the early church, as we see in Acts 2:44–45. Its rigor demanded more than some were willing to give, as we also see in Acts 5, through the tragic story of Ananias and Sapphira. It was not a demand that could be sustained for the church, though it has always attracted Christian radicals and it did indeed get structured into the life of the religious orders.

Where not followed it has often left unease or guilt or transparently desperate efforts at spiritualization—"It's not how much you spend or give but the state of your heart toward your wealth that matters." This common refrain surely is not a fair reading of this text. Christian ethicist Miguel De La Torre responds:

> The author of Luke must have known many would read this passage in such a way as to ignore Jesus' radical call. So in response, Luke gives us, in the very next chapter, the story of Zacchaeus. . . . The rich young ruler asks Jesus what he must do to enter God's reign. Even though he professed to keeping all of God's commandments, Jesus declared that he lacked one thing. He was to sell all his possessions, give the proceeds to the poor, and follow Jesus. Jesus challenged the rich in the hopes that they would find their own salvation through solidarity with the poor. And while the righteous rich young ruler did not, the despised tax collector Zacchaeus did.[7]

---

7. De La Torre, *Politics of Jesús*, 110–11. I note that Zacchaeus promises to give away half, not all, of his possessions (Luke 19:8).

PART TWO

Matthew

10

The Beatitudes

Blessed are the pure in heart, for they will see God.
—MATT 5:8

Texts: Matt 5:1–12/Luke 6:20–26

THE SERMON ON THE Mount (SM) is the largest single block of Jesus' words anywhere in the New Testament (Matt 5:1—7:29). Rich with moral content, it deserves its reputation as the most significant body of moral teachings, not just of Jesus, but of any biblical figure. The SM was central in the moral teaching of the early church, and it continually resurfaces in Christian history, especially when fresh winds of renewal blow through the church. Its moral radicalism continually challenges the church either to a corresponding obedience or to a guilty conscience and strategies of evasion.[1]

Many of the teachings in the SM are unique to Matthew, though some are found in similar form in a shorter parallel passage in Luke 6 (called the Sermon on the Plain). A handful of sayings placed elsewhere in other Gospels also show up in the SM. It is appropriate to note Matthew's role in

---

1. Gushee/Stassen, *Kingdom Ethics*, ch. 5, says more about the unique role of the SM in the history of Christian ethics.

arranging and editing the sayings of Jesus into this powerful collection. It is a work of literary art.

Glen Stassen and I argue in *Kingdom Ethics* that the vast majority of the SM (Matt 5:21—7:11) is an ingenious collection of fourteen "triads," in which Jesus first names a traditional OT teaching about an issue (we call this *traditional righteousness*), then briskly diagnoses a *sinful pattern* of human behavior, and finally offers a *transforming initiative* that can break the sinful pattern and move the practitioner toward an obedience that brings life and peace.[2] This approach contrasts sharply with the "dyadic," "antithetical," "intensification," "hard sayings," or "high ideals" interpretations of the SM, in which Jesus is supposed to have juxtaposed an OT law with his own contradictory, aspirational, highly demanding, even perfectionistic ethical command. The triadic reading of the SM was Glen Stassen's discovery, one of his most important contributions to NT studies and Christian ethics.

Matthew sets up Jesus as a Moses figure, and there are many parallels between the two. Both are men born with special divine purpose, whose lives are threatened from their very beginning, who must flee from or to Egypt, who spend time in the remote wilderness and encounter God there, and who finally ascend a mountain to offer divinely inspired teachings.[3]

The opening statement of the SM (Matt 5:1—12), traditionally called the Beatitudes (from the Latin *beatus*, for blessed), demonstrates considerable continuity with the Jewish tradition. The very formulation: "happy are," "blessed are," is a familiar biblical move (sixty-eight times in the Septuagint[4]), and it is visible especially in the Psalms. Specific blessings offered in Jesus' Beatitudes also seem to have direct or allusive OT precedent (Pss 24, 37, 51, 107; Prov 14:21; Isa 61). The best example is "blessed are the meek, for they will inherit the earth," which is a quotation of the Greek translation of Ps 37:11.

At first glance, the Beatitudes look as if they fall within the wisdom tradition of Israel, and they have often been interpreted as such. That tradition emphasizes the God-given moral structure of the world, teaches character qualities and behaviors that conform with that structure and therefore please God, and promises happiness for those who carefully order their lives accordingly.

---

2. Gushee/Stassen, *Kingdom Ethics*, 95—103.

3. Aaron M. Gale, notes to "The Gospel According to Matthew," in JANT, 19.

4. The Septuagint was the first Greek translation of the Hebrew Bible, undertaken from the third to the first centuries BCE.

Psalm 1 is a great example: "Happy are those who do not follow the advice of the wicked . . . but their delight is the law of the Lord . . . they are like trees planted by streams of water, which yield their fruit in its season." The happy are those who take the wise path of listening to God's law rather than straying into bad company, and this yields the result of a stable, fruitful life over the long term. This is a wisdom teaching.

But I remain persuaded by Glen Stassen's reading of the Beatitudes as a dynamic, participatory, eschatological teaching, rather than a wisdom teaching. Blessed are those who know that today is the day of salvation and who are ready to participate in God's dawning reign! In this interpretation, Stassen was influenced by the earlier work of NT scholars W. D. Davies and Dale Allison.[5]

Wisdom teachings talk about the built-in structure of the universe, with God's direct activity distant, and with what happens to people being the consequences of their own choices. (Sleep all day, and you will starve the next day. Work hard, and you will have plenty to eat. So, get up and work if you don't want to starve.) God sets up a morally ordered world, but it is the natural consequences of our choices that affect our lives. The time horizon is endless, as there is no eschatological vision in wisdom writings.

Jesus is doing something very different in his teaching in the SM, and it is clear from the Beatitudes forward. Jesus came preaching the kingdom of God. That kingdom message declares that God is now intervening, acting decisively to reclaim this broken, rebellious world. The clear connections between Isa 61, the SM, and Jesus' "inaugural address" in Luke 4:16–30 ground this interpretation. Jesus is the fulfillment of the prophecy that God would one day come in power to redeem Israel and the world.[6] God's emissary Jesus is claiming that now is the time. His listeners are being invited right now *to participate in God's kingly deliverance.*

If Jesus comes announcing God's dawning reign, his teaching cannot be primarily about offering timeless wisdom about how to be happy in an endless workaday world. Instead, beginning with the Beatitudes, he is offering a description of the kinds of people who are ready to participate with him in interrupting this timeless, fallen world with deliverance. He is offering a kingdom ethic.

---

5. Davies/Allison Jr., *Matthew*, 436–40. "If Jesus did utter the beatitudes, he must have done so conscious of being the eschatological herald who had been anointed by God and given the Spirit . . . Prophecy has been fulfilled. Eschatology has entered the present" (438–39).

6. Davies/Allison Jr., *Matthew*, 438–39; cf. Culpepper, *Matthew*, 87–88.

Let us briefly consider each of the Beatitudes.

The "poor in spirit" (Matt 5:3) are the humble ones of this world who know their need of God. They are ready and eager for God's kingdom, and not invested in this world's prideful, sinful mini-kingdoms.

"Those who mourn" (Matt 5:4) are not just those sad over their losses but instead those who grieve over their own and their community's sins, who weep for a better world. They are the opposite of those who see this world from the heights of privilege and do so with complacency.

"The meek" (Matt 5:5) are those who trust God to deliver them, even from great need, rather than claiming their rights or abusing their opportunity to take what they want or need.[7]

"Those who hunger and thirst for righteousness" (*dikaiosynē*—Matt 5:6), better translated into English as "justice," are those who earnestly desire the justice, the right-relatedness, the right-making, that will be a part of God's reign. These are hungry for what God is hungry for and Jesus is about to do, rather than being fine with this world's rank injustice.

"The merciful" (Matt 5:7) have compassionate hearts which reflect the very mercy of God that motivates God's deliverance of suffering humanity—and like God they act on their compassion, in a world full of cruel indifference.

"The pure in heart" (Matt 5:8) are best understood as those with singleness of purpose—to do God's will and to live into God's reign. They are not distracted by the various human projects that reflect indifference to or direct rebellion against God's will.

"The peacemakers" (Matt 5:9) are blessed because they resemble God in seeking to end all human violence and conflict, rather than participating in humanity's endless cycles of violence. Peace is a key mark of the kingdom.

"Those who are persecuted for righteousness' sake" (Matt 5:10–12) are not the smarmy self-righteous, but those willing to pay a price to build God's reign, against the opposition of violence, greed, and exclusion. This Beatitude speaks to the inevitable conflict and suffering that come to those who take their stand for God's "upside-down kingdom."

In Luke's version (Luke 6:20–26), the blessed are quite simply the poor, hungry, weeping, hated, and excluded. Matthew's version subtly shifts attention from the recipient's material condition to their spiritual condition. But Jewish tradition had long put the concepts together, as Davies and

7. Bonhoeffer, *Discipleship*, 105.

Allison put it in relation to the first Beatitude: "They knew the meaning of need because they were poor in spirit and poor in fact."[8]

The "woes" are proclaimed to those who sit on top of this world now—for their positions are soon to be reversed by God's decisive intervention. But as with the blessings, it is not just their exalted material position and status that leads to Jesus proclaiming judgment over them, but the closely connected spiritual and moral maladies, such as trust in riches and indifference to the poor.

Matthew's beatitudes, slightly softer, offer words of affirmation and promise of divine reward for a newly forming community poised in readiness for the reign of God. It is as if Jesus is saying: *Here on this mountain, I have found my team for God's kingdom. I celebrate them, and now I will get them ready for the hard but beautiful work that lies ahead.* Here we see the church that lives for the kingdom of God being assembled.

8. Davies/Allison Jr., *Matthew*, 443; Culpepper, *Matthew*, 89, concurs with this judgment.

11

Let Your Light Shine

Let your light shine before others, so that they may see your good works and give glory to your Father in heaven.

—*MATT 5:16*

I have come not to abolish but to fulfill . . . unless your righteousness exceeds that of the scribes and Pharisees, you will never enter the kingdom.

—*MATT 5:17, 20*

Text: Matt 5:13–20/Luke 14:34–35

JESUS SAYS TO HIS followers that they are the "salt of the earth" and the "light of the world." These are memorable images that became engrained in the Christian tradition. But that does not mean we have a clear understanding of what Jesus meant. This takes some effort.[1]

We can begin by clarifying that the "you" here is in the plural and should be understood as those who are committed to following Jesus' way

---

1. Gushee/Stassen, *Kingdom Ethics*, 196–201, offers an exposition of Matt 5:13–16, followed closely below.

as the authoritative interpreter of God's will and agent of the kingdom. The "you" here is not just everyone, but instead the renewed Jewish-messianic-kingdom community that Jesus is now forming.

"Salt of the earth" does not mean, as in the English vernacular, good solid country folk. It goes back to an ancient Mesopotamian notion of salt as symbolizing purity and wisdom (cf. Exod 30:35, 2 Kgs 2:19–23, Ezek 16:4).[2] The Hebrew Bible also used salt in association with covenant loyalty (Lev 2:13, Num 18:19), as an element added to sacrifices (Lev 2:13), as a seasoning for food (Job 6:6), and for other purposes. We tend to think of salt's use as a preservative, but that does not appear in the Bible.[3]

There are several references to salt in the NT, and the image is, again, not used in just one way (cf. Mark 9:49–50, Col 4:6, Jas 3:12). Luke 14:34–35 parallels Matt 5:13, though it adds references to salting the soil and manure.

W. D. Davies argued, and *Kingdom Ethics* agrees, that the imagery of salt likely was drawn from an example available very close at hand—the Qumran community, gathered by the extremely salty Dead Sea.[4] This separatist Jewish community, which we have mentioned earlier, sought to live morally and ritually pure lives, by setting themselves radically apart from a mainstream Jewish community that it considered corrupt.

Jesus next offers a warning that helps clarify his meaning: "But if salt has lost its taste, how can its saltiness be restored? It is no longer good for anything" (Matt 5:13). If we think of non-kingdom existence as bland, insipid, and tasteless, we may have a start on Jesus' use of this image here. Jesus "salted" this world by his kingdom-bringing presence, and his followers are to resemble him in our "salty" flavor, "tasted" through our striking obedience to the radical way of life in which he is instructing us. On the other hand, those who claim to be God's people who live according to the world's rules rather than God's rules are, in Jesus' words, good for nothing.

Thus far, Jesus appears to be tracking with the radical purism of the Qumran community. Then he says, "You are the light of the world" (Matt 5:14). This language also connects to Qumran, in that this community

---

2. Gale, in JANT, 19.

3. Gushee/Stassen, *Kingdom Ethics*, 197. Culpepper, *Matthew*, 100, offers further discussion of the OT usages of salt in reality and metaphor.

4. Gushee/Stassen, *Kingdom Ethics*, 196–97, citing Davies, *Setting of the Sermon on the Mount*, 214.

spoke of itself as "the sons of light," living on the side of God, who opposed "the sons of darkness."[5]

Consistently in the Bible, God is symbolized as light and as bringing light (Gen 1:3; Ps 119:105; Prov 6:23; Isa 2:5, 9:2–7, 42:6, 49:6, 60:19; Dan 12:3). God is light, and God brings light into the world that humans and Satan have made so dark.

Jesus, in turn, is the light of the world, the one who shines in the darkness, and the darkness has not, and cannot, overcome it (John 1:4–5). But here is where Jesus breaks with Qumran.[6] We are not to hide our light under a bushel basket (Matt 5:15). We should be *visible* as God's light: "Let your light shine before others, that they may see your good works and give glory to your Father in heaven" (Matt 5:16). We cannot be light in the world if we go off and hide.

The Greek word being translated here as "they may see" is *horaō*. *Horaō* carries with it a spiritual connotation, more like the English words "perceive" or "discern." It can also be reasonably translated as "experience." How we let our light shine is by living in such a way that people see (perceive, discern, experience) our good works, and that motivates them to give glory to God.

In *Kingdom Ethics*, we call this teaching a "salt, light, and deeds" triad.[7] It is in our deeds of obedience to Jesus that we function as salt and light. Through our lives we point people to God so clearly that they honor God's name because of what they have seen in us.

In short, followers of Jesus constitute an alternative community (salt), living toward the reign of God, distinct from the world but engaged in a caring, constructive way within the world (light), with our deeds of obedience to Christ the greatest evidence of our identity and of God's glory.

Jesus goes on to say, "Do not think that I have come to abolish the Law or the Prophets; I have come not to abolish but to fulfill" (Matt 5:17).

The Greek words for "abolish" (*katalysai*) and "fulfill" (*plērōsai*) rhyme. Jesus liked to have fun with his words and picked them intentionally. There are multiple examples of rhyming in the Hebrew tradition. The writers of the Greek NT sometimes adapted Jesus' Aramaic rhymes into Greek ones. Perhaps Jesus is engaging in this sort of theatrical rhetoric, either for the sake of impact, or to make these words easier for his audience to remember.

5. Gale, in JANT, 19.

6. Gushee/Stassen, *Kingdom Ethics*, 199, following Davies.

7. Gushee/Stassen, *Kingdom Ethics*, 201.

It was common for the Hebrew Bible's content to be summarized as "the Law and the Prophets." Teaching up on a mountain, like Moses did at Mt. Sinai, Jesus refuses to declare himself an abolisher of the Law of Moses or of the prophets whose main job was to exhort Israel to keep God's Law truly.

He says he came not to abolish but to fulfill the Law. This is a crucial claim. It reflects a major argument in the first century about Jesus and later the church's relationship, not just to the OT canon and Jewish Law, but also to the Jewish tradition and the Jewish people. Tensions between Jewish Christians and gentile Christians over Torah observance are apparent in the New Testament itself, and helped to create what became a tragic anti-Jewish trajectory in Christian theology.[8]

Matthew's Jesus offers a better way. Jesus here claims that all teachings he will offer represent a fulfillment rather than a negation of Jewish Law. It makes sense when you watch what he does in the rest of the Sermon on the Mount.

For example, soon he will affirm the Decalogue teachings about not murdering, not committing adultery, not lying, not stealing, not coveting. But he will go on to teach about both how we end up on the path toward doing these bad things, and how to get off that path before it is too late. This is not a teaching that abolishes the Law, but instead reveals how to obey it from the heart, and with a strategy that might just change the dynamics taking us down the wrong path.

Jesus sternly warns against any loosening or weakening of God's Law. His goal is not to set aside God's will but to do it, obey it, and teach it to others.

Finally, he says, "Unless your righteousness exceeds that of the scribes and Pharisees, you will never enter the kingdom" (Matt 5:20).

Like the Jewish prophets before him, Jesus saw around him examples of a kind of righteousness that didn't measure up to what he believed that God really wanted. It wasn't characteristic of everybody, but it was visible in some of those who ended up competing with him to define God's will and God's way.

This righteousness was too focused on minute details of the Law and missed weightier priorities like love, justice, mercy, and faithfulness (Matt 23:23). It was a righteousness that focused too much on what not to do and not enough on what to do.

While we need to be aware of later tensions affecting how the Gospel writers present Jesus' relationship with his Jewish interlocutors, it does

8. Bibliowicz, *Jewish-Christian Relations.*

seem that Jesus represented a highly demanding prophetic moral vision that was impatient with certain directions of piety and practice that he saw around him. Like all the Jewish prophets, he wanted to call the people to the deepest meaning of Torah, as he understood it.

Already, Jesus has quickened the heartbeats of his listeners by proclaiming that God's kingdom is dawning. He has pronounced blessings on those whose character, heart, motives, way of life, and need show that they are ready for the change that is coming—and ready to be a part of it.

Now he is telling a coalescing community of followers more about their role. They are to become a distinctive remnant community, salt of the earth and light of the world, a transformative presence of God in the world. They are to meet and exceed the behavioral requirements of Torah, though in a manner different from the Pharisees. Through their actions, they are to bear witness to the new work that God is doing, and to inspire people to give glory to God.

Two thousand years later, this vision of what it means to be the church should remain compelling to Christians.

12

Making Peace

You have heard that it was said to those of ancient times, "You shall not murder," and "whoever murders shall be liable to judgment." But I say to you that if you are angry with a brother or sister, you will be liable to judgment, and if you insult a brother or sister, you will be liable to the council, and if you say, "You fool," you will be liable to the hell of fire. So when you are offering your gift at the altar, if you remember that your brother or sister has something against you, leave your gift there before the altar and go; first be reconciled to your brother or sister, and then come and offer your gift.

—MATT 5:21–24

Texts: Matt 5:21–26/Luke 12:57–59

GENERATIONS OF CHRISTIANS WERE taught a dyadic, antithetical, intensification, hard sayings, or high ideals interpretation, not just of this passage but of the entire Sermon on the Mount. I introduced this idea in ch. 10, but want to develop it further as we move into the crucial next section of the SM.

Dyadic/antithetical means something has two parts, the second contrasting with the first: 1) "You have heard," 2) "But I say." For Matt 5:21–48, that is an obvious place to start, of course, because Jesus does use that language to start off each of the next six teachings. But this has been taken to mean that Jesus is dismissing the inferior Jewish Law and replacing it with his own authoritative, antithetical new teaching. That conclusion, Glen Stassen and I have argued, is not warranted.[1]

Intensification means that Jesus goes further than the OT command. He does not dismiss Torah but does teach a more intense, more rigorous version of it: You were taught not to murder, and now I teach that it is just as wrong to be angry with someone as it is to kill them.

Hard sayings or high ideals means that Jesus teaches very hard things, offering an aspirational ethic, pretty much impossible, an ideal to strive for but always beyond our reach. Here that ethic would be that his followers should aspire never to be angry with people. It was long argued in Christian theology that one reason Jesus offered a pretty much impossible ethic was to drive us to our knees in repentance and gratitude for the forgiving grace of God.

One other option, less often named but often in the air, has been to read Jesus as offering what might be called an *interiorization* of Jewish Law. The idea is that Jesus cares about the state of our hearts, the deepest recesses of our motives, thoughts, and feelings. Indeed, he cares so much that from his perspective murderous thoughts toward someone are *no different from,* or *just as bad as,* murderous actions.

In various ways, each of these amount to Jesus offering a *radical perfectionist* ethic that soars above, or burrows deeper, than traditional norms—not just in Jewish Law but in all legal systems and moral codes ever developed by human communities.[2] Reinhold Niebuhr was one ethicist who read Jesus in this way, in the end finding his teachings breathtaking and admirable, but impossible.[3]

When we read this teaching about anger in a perfectionist way, all kinds of problems immediately emerge.

1. Gushee/Stassen, *Kingdom Ethics,* ch. 5. Davies/Allison Jr., *Matthew,* 506–7, argue that Jesus offers a "contrast" but not a "contradiction" of Torah, and that "anyone who followed the words of Jesus in Matt 5:21–48 would not find himself in violation of any Jewish law."

2. E. P. Sanders is just one example of a NT scholar who argued that Jesus offers an "idealistic perfectionist" ethic. See Sanders, *Historical Figure of Jesus,* ch. 13.

3. Niebuhr, *An Interpretation of Christian Ethics.* Niebuhr, who liked paradox, described Jesus' radical love ethic as the "impossible possibility." *Interpretation of Christian Ethics,* 72.

For example, it appears that Jesus is teaching that it is always wrong to get angry. Always? No anger is ever justified?

The problem is so immediately obvious that some Greek NT manuscripts as early as the third century added *eike*, "without cause," to this text (Matt 5:22), though that is by no means the majority textual reading. Dietrich Bonhoeffer described this textual amendment as "the first cautious limitation of the sting of Jesus' words," and he rejected it.

Bonhoeffer himself takes a perfectionist reading—"there is no distinction between so-called just anger and unjust anger."[4] But not only can most of us think of examples in which we have become angry for quite a good cause, we can easily remember times when Jesus himself spoke and acted with anger, as when he cleared the temple (see ch. 38 below).

At first glance, Jesus seems to be equating anger and murder, treating anger as just as liable to divine judgment as murder.[5] But surely there is a moral difference between a flash of anger in our hearts, or even in our words (Matt 5:22) and a purposeful gunshot to the head. Being able to contain ourselves, to set limits on our actions, to draw firm lines between angry thoughts and violent deeds, is fundamental to morality—so fundamental that we teach it urgently to our children. We must be able to maintain a moral distinction between anger and murder.

Glen Stassen was impressed by these problems, and his pioneering *transforming initiatives* interpretation of the SM—beginning here in Matt 5 with the six so-called "antitheses"—offers what I still believe is a better way forward.[6]

Stassen argued that these teachings should be read as triads: traditional righteousness, followed by a sinful pattern, and concluding with a transforming initiative.

Let's try it out. In this text, the traditional teachings are "You shall not murder" and "whoever murders shall be subject to judgment" (Matt 5:21). Matthew 5 and the Greek Septuagint translation of Exod 20:13 in the Ten Commandments use the same word for murder, *phoneuseis*. Jesus is clearly quoting from the Decalogue. Jesus respected Jewish Law and treated

4. Bonhoeffer, *Discipleship*, 122.

5. Davies/Allison Jr., *Matthew*, 521, make this move. They argue Jesus was equating anger with murder. They also argue that Jesus makes no allowance for justified anger. I disagree, as I think Jesus was teaching about how to overcome sinful patterns of anger that can lead to the greater wrong of violence, even murder.

6. NT scholar Alan Culpepper, *Matthew*, 106–21, agrees, explicitly accepting the Stassen transforming initiatives interpretation of Matt 5:21–48.

it seriously. Here he demonstrates that. He does not abrogate or in any way disrespect these traditional teachings against murder.

Stassen reads Matt 5:22 as an escalating pattern of anger, and thus as a sinful pattern. First, we get angry, then we hurl an insult, then we deride the intelligence or character of the other person by calling them a fool. Assume a public setting for this and it gets even more intense.

In any culture, there are recognized ways that escalating anger and disrespect in a human conflict are communicated by verbal and nonverbal signs. All of us have watched this happen, and we know that by the time the angry signs and words get harsh enough the fists and weapons may not be far away. In the gun-toting US culture, it is almost always the better part of wisdom to back away from a fight long before the weapons come out.

Jesus' breakthrough is to offer a transforming initiative to address this sinful pattern. That breakthrough is offered in Matt 5:23–24 and then reinforced in Matt 5:25–26. It is to prioritize making peace so highly that even if one is in a sacred act of religious devotion—making an offering at the temple—that act must be suspended to seek peace in a human relationship. It is as if God is not interested in our worship if we are not interested in healing our broken relationships.

Stassen noted that all the imperative verbs in the passage are found in Matt 5:23–24: remember, leave, go, be reconciled, come, offer your gift. His conclusion was that the answer to escalating patterns of anger is to take transforming initiatives to make peace.

It is interesting that verses 25–26 find a parallel in Luke 12:57–59, where the teaching stands alone and is rather clearly focused on avoiding litigation. In his editorial artistry, Matthew drafts that stand-alone nugget of teaching and places it into service here—where it seems to be intended as a stern warning of divine judgment for not making peace.

In sum, the triadic reading of this text goes like this: God commanded in the OT that we not kill each other. The way people end up killing each other (often) is by letting unresolved anger escalate to insults and violence. What we can do about this is *not* to try *really, really hard to never get angry*, but instead to make a practice of paying attention to unreconciled relationships and unresolved anger, and to *take active initiatives to go and make peace*. When we surprise people with requests for conversation-toward-peace, we can actively de-escalate conflict and move toward its resolution. This is what God really wants—a practice of peacemaking. After all, peace is part of the reign of God that Jesus came to bring. Notice that this interpretation shifts the focus away from solely inward-looking moral perfectionism and toward "a restoration of relationships."[7]

Let me conclude by complicating matters with a return to the "don't be angry" reading of this passage. It has an enduring attraction that must not be dismissed. Anger is not especially pleasant, and people grow weary of seething in its cauldron. Many self-help books, many counselors, many religious and philosophical traditions, and many everyday Christians seek paths to inner peace, self-mastery, and victory over negative emotions. It is wearisome to be routinely riled up by what other people do. It would be pure freedom to be so self-directing, so emotionally balanced, and perhaps so empowered by God's Spirit, that we could rise above what other people do to us.

On the other hand, numerous voices from historically oppressed groups have argued strongly for, as my teacher Beverly Harrison once put it, "the power of anger in the work of love."[8] The beat-up and bullied, the marginalized and dispossessed, naturally feel anger at those who mistreat them. As Howard Thurman argued, this anger toward those who mistreat us—even if experienced as "hate"—"becomes a device by which an individual seeks to protect himself against moral disintegration . . . for the weak, hatred seems to serve a creative purpose."[9] The basic insight here is that anger is a natural response to mistreatment, an essential self-validation of one's God-given dignity, and even an empowering source of reparative action for justice.

Thurman went on, however, to conclude that "hatred destroys finally the life of the hater . . . Jesus rejected hatred because he saw that hatred meant death."[10] Anger has motivated many to push back against injustice, and such efforts have often led to social change campaigns that have made the world a better place. But anger, if allowed to harden into hate, brings death to the hater and the hated—which takes us back in the direction of Jesus' teaching of transforming initiatives that can ultimately bring reconciliation to broken relationships.

7. Culpepper, *Matthew*, 109.

8. Harrison, "Power of Anger in the Work of Love." Harrison writes, "Anger is not the opposite of love . . . Anger is a mode of connectedness to others and it is always a vivid form of caring," 14.

9. Thurman, *Jesus and the Disinherited*, 72, 75.

10. Thurman, *Jesus and the Disinherited*, 76–78.

13

Preventing Adultery

Everyone who looks at a woman with lust has already committed adultery with her in his heart.

—MATT 5:28

Texts: Matt 5:27–30, cf. Mark 9:43–48/Matt 18:8–9

MOICHEIA IS THE GREEK word used here to translate Jesus' teaching on adultery. According to the *Women's Bible Commentary*, in Greek culture the word *moicheia* "connoted illicit intercourse with 'respectable women,' and thus indicated a violation of their honor; it did not apply to relations with slaves or prostitutes."[1] Meanwhile, under Israelite law, "the prohibition of adultery (Exod 20:14, Deut 5:18) means 'You shall not have sexual intercourse with a fellow Israelite's wife.'"[2] But this obligation was really owed to the other male Israelite, respecting his property rights, not to his own wife, respecting their marriage covenant. Jesus will not be satisfied with either of these patriarchal ethical formulas.

In the last chapter we already set the options for interpreting what Jesus is saying in the six sayings of Matt 5:21–48: dyadic/antithetical,

1. Amy-Jill Levine, "Gospel of Matthew," in *Women's Bible Commentary*, 470.
2. Culpepper, *Matthew*, 110.

intensification, hard sayings, high ideals, and interiorization could be grouped together as a "radical perfectionist" vision, whereas the transforming initiatives reading was Glen Stassen's helpful alternative.

As we take up Jesus' teaching about adultery, we face the same options. Jesus could be read as offering a dyadic antithesis: whereas OT Law banned adultery, he bans lust. Or he intensifies the ban on adultery to a ban on even a lustful look or thought. Or he offers the impossibly hard saying/high ideal that one must never have even a passing lustful thought. Or he does a radical interiorization move to say that a lustful thought or feeling is no different from, and just as bad as, committing physical adultery.

In *Kingdom Ethics*, we attempted to take the hyperbolic plucking out of eyes and cutting off hands as a kind of transforming initiative.[3] Our reading there went something like this:

Traditional Righteousness: You shall not commit adultery. Jesus affirms this traditional teaching, the seventh commandment.

Sinful Pattern: Developing a habit of dwelling on lustful thoughts toward someone not your spouse. This could extend to developing patterns of inappropriate emotional, proximal, or physical intimacy that could constitute the path to adultery. Jesus refuses to allow distinctions related to the marital status of the woman whom the man might be lusting after.

Transforming Initiative: Cut off habits of viewing persons as objects, or of using hands wrongly (as in masturbating to lustful images or thoughts of someone not your spouse). The maiming language is hyperbolic, signaling that sexual self-discipline and the ban on adultery really matter to God.[4]

Jesus is saying that just as the ban on murder in the Ten Commandments still holds, so does the ban on adultery. Murder is unjust killing, and adultery is unjust sex. Just as murder is clearly wrong according to God's command, so is adultery. And adultery now means having sex with anyone who is not your spouse.

I do not believe that Jesus is saying that anytime we feel attracted to the beauty, personality, or character of another person, it is the same thing as having sex with them. Many have loaded themselves with guilt because they were taught this. It is easy to see how the radical perfectionist reading of this passage gets you there.

The Greek here can plausibly be translated "anyone who looks at a woman *to desire her*," e.g., with lustful intent, and that helps quite a bit. On

3. Gushee/Stassen, *Kingdom Ethics*, 255–60.
4. Davies/Allison Jr., *Matthew*, 524.

the one hand, there is the passing spark of attraction, a biochemical firing of the neurons that simply is a part of being human and that moves the species forward one generation after another. On the other hand, there is the purposeful cultivation of an attraction that is morally forbidden. These are not the same thing.

Why does any of this matter? Haven't we left all this moral puritanism behind long ago?

Christianity once had a reputation for being an ascetic, killjoy religion. Everything fun seemed to be against the rules. In my Baptist church in high school, that included card playing, R-rated movies, dancing, alcohol, cursing, and sex. The only vices allowed were to drink way too much sweet tea and eat way too much covered-dish supper. So, everyone was sober, but no one's clothes fit very well.

And of course, the Protestant version of Christian asceticism was a pale imitation of an older Catholic tradition that was much stricter. If you felt called to the highest path of religious devotion, you became a priest, monk, or nun. And these folks gave up pretty much all the main earthly pleasures, for their whole lives. They gave up their freedom, they gave up money, and they gave up sex—of course, they did so in pursuit of God, the highest good.

Protestants used to love to make fun of what we described as Catholic legalism—which we rejected because, after all, we were "not under law but under grace." But quite often we reconstructed our own forms of legalism later, which we did not recognize as legalism because it didn't involve priests, monks, and nuns.

But then, some years later, many in all kinds of Christian communities sloughed off legalism so profoundly that we forgot that Christ made any moral demands on us at all. The sexual misconduct of both everyday Christians and Christian leaders grew to staggering levels. And Christians stopped caring about whether public figures demonstrated anything as old-fashioned as covenant fidelity in marriage.

So today it appears timely to remind ourselves of some reasons why both the Decalogue and the Sermon on the Mount banned adultery, and why that ban still makes sense millennia later, even if much has changed in our understanding of marriage and arrangement of power relations therein.

Adultery was banned in the Decalogue in part to secure the well-being of children. Men are much more likely to care for their long-dependent young if they are confident that the children that their wives bear are their own. The broader meaning here was to secure family lineage across many generations.

Adultery was banned in the Decalogue in part because wives were understood to belong to their husbands in a quasi-property sense. The sense of property and "ownership" was not reciprocal because of patriarchy. Polygamy offers an obvious example of the nonexclusive, patriarchal understanding of women as sexual property. But today we can move past patriarchy and recognize a kind of proprietary right to sexual exclusivity in marriage. It is stated whenever spouses affirm to each other, "You belong to me, and I belong to you."

Adultery was banned in the Decalogue and more broadly in the Hebrew Bible in part due to a developing sense of marriage as a covenant (see Mal 3). Spouses exchanged sacred vows with each other, in community, and before God. It is clear already in the OT that sexual exclusivity was understood to be part of their vow. Just as Israel must practice covenant fidelity with its one God, so spouses must do the same with each other. I address marriage as a covenant in several of my works.[5] This concept is desperately in need of retrieval and strengthening.

I am convinced that adultery was banned by Jesus in part to protect women from being abandoned by roving-eye husbands (see ch. 8 above). If men are free to commit adultery or abandon their wives for the newer model (even if that abandonment is legal and is called "divorce"), women are highly vulnerable. That is especially salient in any society in which women lack equal economic power to men, which remains the situation in many places even now.

Adultery should be understood to be banned today because of the unitive power and emotional vulnerability of sex. Sexual intercourse is the ultimate physical intimacy. Of its nature it connects persons and not just bodies. It reveals and deepens vulnerability. One reason adultery is banned is because it stomps on that vulnerability. One reason we know that matters is because of how enraged and wounded people become when they discover their spouse has been unfaithful.

Maintaining steady, happy, long-term covenantal-marital relationships is hard. Much more is at stake when children are a part of the picture. Faithfulness in marriage is a crucial part of protecting the marriage covenant, the bedrock of family life and a key to the well-being of both adults and children.

5. Cf. Gushee, *Getting Marriage Right*, ch. 6.

14

Telling the Truth

Let your word be "Yes, Yes" or "No, No"; anything more than this comes from the evil one.

—MATT 5:37

Texts: Matt 5:33–37, cf. Matt 23:16–22

AN OATH IS A verbal declaration appealing to a god, or something else sacred, that is made to demonstrate and guarantee that one is speaking the truth or will keep a promise. Such oaths may be taken on personal initiative or as a part of a religious, legal, or cultural system.

A person may say, "I swear to God that I will never tell a soul about what just happened to me." When she does, she is assuring the listener of her future behavior through the strength of a solemn promise to/before God.

In US courts, officers require that we raise our right hands and assent to some version of this statement: "Do you swear that the evidence you shall give to the court in this matter shall be the truth, the whole truth, and nothing but the truth, so help you God?" Courts require this because the truth matters so much in legal testimony. Courts reinforce the power of the oath through threat of legal sanction if it is violated.

The Hebrew Bible reveals the existence of regular practices of oath-taking and vow-making in the name of God.[1] Indeed, in a few legal contexts it not only permits but even mandates oaths (see Exod 22:10–11; Deut 6:13, 10:20). It also offers urgent warnings against "swearing falsely," which Jesus cites here in Matt 5:33. Consider Lev 19:12: "You shall not swear falsely by my name, profaning the name of the Lord your God." This command is integrated with several commands related to social and moral relations in the covenant community.

To swear falsely, or not to keep one's oaths, appears to be an example of *dealing falsely* (Lev 19:11), and it is connected in the surrounding verses in Leviticus 19 to stealing, lying, and defrauding. At its best, the practice of vowing, oath-taking, or swearing in God's name was intended to reinforce the absoluteness of the moral obligations that Jews had both to neighbor and to God.

Why would Jesus have any problem with this, then? Why does he rule it out, absolutely and entirely? In this passage and in Matt 23:16–22, Jesus appears to be offering a window into vowing practices that had developed into an elaborate casuistry of the relative binding power of specific oaths, which seemed to him to have devolved to a systematized religious trickery. Jesus describes all of this as taking God's name in vain; it also harms neighbor and community by undercutting the trustworthiness not just of oaths but of all speech.

In the Matt 5 text, Jesus appears simply to ban all vow-making and oath-taking. In one of his more memorable short sayings, he says, "Let your word be 'Yes, Yes,' or No, No'" (Matt 5:37).

The narrowest reading of Jesus' intent here would be that he believed the elaborate vowing/oathing practices around him were weakening truth-telling in the Jewish community, with the problem grossly exacerbated by the fact that this was being done with religious sanction.

The antidote, the transforming initiative, is to tell the truth simply and straightforwardly, all the time, without recourse to oaths or vows. When you say yes, mean it; when you say no, mean that. A truthful person does

---

1. In ancient Jewish practice, there were two main categories of this type: vows and oaths. Each receives a tractate in the Mishnah, the first part of the Talmud. In an "assertive oath," the oath-taker swears by God, or invokes divine judgment, to guarantee that they have or have not done something. In a "promissory oath," the person swears that they will or will not do something. A vow appears to be distinct from an oath in having this formula: "O Lord, if you will . . . I will . . ."), though "the difference between vows and oaths is not unambiguous." Culpepper, *Matthew*, 114.

not need backup swearing either to make themselves tell the truth or to be believed when they make a promise: "Be a person of such integrity that oaths are unnecessary."[2]

Dietrich Bonhoeffer weighed in on the paradoxical problem created by making oaths to tell the truth:

> The oath is proof of the existence of lies in the world. If human beings could not lie, oaths would not be necessary. Thus an oath is a barrier against lying. But in providing this, it also encourages lying, for whenever an oath claims final truthfulness for itself, then at the same time room is also given for lying to take place; a certain right of existence is granted to the lie. Old Testament law uses oaths to reject lying. But Jesus rejects lying by prohibiting oaths.[3]

In *Jesus and the Disinherited*, Howard Thurman offers a bracing discussion of truthfulness and deception from the perspective of the powerless. He emphasizes how very difficult it is to tell the truth when you are an oppressed person. Thurman says that the disinherited of the earth learn practices of deception to ensure their own survival: "Deception is perhaps the oldest of all the techniques by which the weak have protected themselves against the strong."[4] One can think of many sad examples—abused children, spouses, workers, citizens, journalists, and so on.

But after describing practices of lying for survival, Thurman ultimately concludes that these corrode and degrade the soul of the deceivers: "The penalty of deception is to *become* a deception, with all sense of moral discrimination vitiated. A man who lies habitually becomes a lie, and it is increasingly impossible for him to know when he is lying and when he is not."[5]

Certain that Jesus was addressing subjugated people who were living under oppression, Thurman concludes that Jesus' teaching here on simply telling the truth was intended as part of the path of dignity and resistance. Even if one's life is risked by telling the truth, it is still better than the degradation of having to tell lies day after day to survive. "[B]e simply, directly truthful, whatever may be the cost in life, limb, or security."[6] Not every ethi-

---

2. Culpepper, *Matthew*, 116.

3. Bonhoeffer, *Discipleship*, 129. Davies/Allison Jr., *Matthew*, 533: "When the truth reigns, 'that mighty god, the oath . . . is dethroned, being without utility.'"

4. Thurman, *Jesus and the Disinherited*, 48.

5. Thurman, *Jesus and the Disinherited*, 55.

6. Thurman, *Jesus and the Disinherited*, 60.

cist agrees with the principle—or at least with imposing absolutism about truth-telling on oppressed people—but it make sense at a very deep level.[7]

Thurman's courageous counsel here does indeed make us think of Jesus' own fearless, truth-telling way of life, in all circumstances. While Jesus did not always directly answer queries intended to trick him, he never lied in response. Sometimes he held his tongue, sometimes he deflected a question with a different return question. But he never lied to live another day. And, not incidentally, he never used a sacred vow to reinforce the significance or truth of his words.

Jesus' teaching here has been taken in a legalist direction by some Christians who have understood it to mean that they cannot take a sacred vow, in court for example. So, they "affirm" rather than "swear" to tell the truth. This move has a very long tradition.[8] But it misses the point of this teaching, which is about developing the fearless practice of telling the truth in everyday life—and not making a tool of the holy name of God to get yourself to tell the truth and to get others to believe you.

I wonder if Jesus' teaching about vows and oaths is not only about truth, but also about how to look at the future in a life of fidelity to God. What if Jesus is trying to teach his listeners to take each moment as it comes and to ask what God is requiring in that moment? Those oaths made *in advance* to do X or refrain from doing Y presume reliable advance knowledge of what it will be desirable for us to do in a future that only God knows. As Bonhoeffer writes, "Because Christians never control their future, a solemn promise under oath . . . is fraught with greatest danger for them."[9] Rather than making an oath that might one day need to be retracted for circumstantial reasons, perhaps it is best to respond to God and neighbor moment by moment.

The Epistle of James, which bans swearing (Jas 5:12) in a direct echo of Jesus' teaching here, also teaches against making any declarations as to our plans for the next day: "You do not even know what tomorrow will bring. What is your life? For you are a mist that appears for a little while and then vanishes" (Jas 5:14). For James, making declarations about our plans for the future is a form of boasting. Instead, we are to sit loosely with

---

7. See Gushee/Stassen, *Kingdom Ethics*, ch. 15, for more on this issue.

8. Davies/Allison Jr., *Matthew*, 535.

9. Bonhoeffer, *Discipleship*, 130. He wrote in a context in which the regime required state employees, including church officials, to swear oaths of loyalty to the Nazi government and eventually to the person of Adolf Hitler.

plans and trust God's will for what happens next. Maybe Jesus' problem with oath-taking is not just the temptation to lie under its cover, but also the temptation to think that the future is ours to plan, rather than God's to orchestrate and ours to respond. Maybe this is a teaching about pride, and not just about truth.

15

Loving Enemies

But I say to you: Do not resist an evildoer. But if anyone strikes you on the right cheek, turn the other also.

—MATT 5:39

But I say to you: Love your enemies and pray for those who persecute you.

—MATT 5:44

Texts: Matt 5:38–48/Luke 6:27–36

THE CHOICE BETWEEN READING Jesus as offering a radical perfectionist ethic versus an ethic of transforming initiatives is never starker than in these back-to-back passages exhorting listeners to turn the other cheek and love their enemies.

This time let's start with the transforming initiatives reading and see if it is plausible.

In Matt 5:38–42, the traditional righteousness is rendered as "an eye for an eye and a tooth for a tooth." Yes, that teaching, the principle of *lex talionis*, is clearly found in the OT (Exod 21:23–25; Lev 24:19–21; Deut 19:21). It is always helpful to point out that an eye for an eye means *proportionate retribution*, which was an advance in justice over escalatory retribution, the latter being so common, and so dangerous, when people are angry and aggrieved (cf. Gen 4:23–24).[1] Escalating retribution definitely can become a sinful pattern. But Jesus appeared to view even proportionate retribution as both the traditional righteousness and the sinful pattern.[2]

Jesus offers a transforming initiative here most clearly if the Greek normally rendered "do not resist an evildoer" is interpreted as meaning "we should not be retaliating revengefully against evil or by evil means."[3] That makes it a teaching against revenge, but not a teaching against resisting evil. This move has been crucial for reading this teaching as a transforming initiative, and more broadly for viewing it as a strategic part of nonviolent resistance rather than pure nonresistance.[4]

Consider the specific dynamics of the event Jesus describes here. To be struck on the right cheek with a right hand almost certainly means a backhanded slap. Try it out (in your mind only, please!) and you will see it. A backhanded slap struck in public is not part of a slugfest but instead an act intended to humiliate.[5] Jesus is saying that we should respond to such an insulting blow not by retaliating in kind but by positioning our body to offer the left cheek. Why? It halts the escalation of violence, retains the offended one's dignity, and asks the aggressor whether he really wants to escalate the fight by closing his fist and striking a full-on blow to the left cheek.[6]

---

1. Culpepper, *Matthew*, 116, points out that this principle is found in the ancient Code of Hammurabi, which predates the Pentateuch, and "was a step toward limiting unrestrained violence."

2. Gushee/Stassen, *Kingdom Ethics*, 219, puts it this way: "If the Old Testament teaching of 'life for life' is understood as a command to limit revenge by killing only the killer and not the killer's family . . . then Jesus was here taking a further leap in the same direction, limiting murderous revenge all the way down to zero. Jesus opposed taking a life as retribution for a life."

3. Gushee/Stassen, *Kingdom Ethics*, 219.

4. The distinction must be precisely drawn—*Kingdom Ethics* argues that Jesus taught *nonviolent resistance* to evil and evildoers, not nonresistance. This is not accurately captured in a statement like this in Culpepper, *Matthew*, 117: "The admonition is broad: do not oppose or resist the evildoer." When Gandhi challenged British colonialism, or King led civil rights marchers, that was nonviolent resistance to evil, not nonresistance to evil.

5. Culpepper, *Matthew*, 117, and Davies/Allison Jr., *Matthew*, 543, concur with this reading.

6. Gale, in JANT, 21, puts it well in saying that turning the other cheek is a response "with neither violence nor abjection."

Jesus goes on with two examples of responding nonviolently to legally sanctioned harms—to give up not only coat but cloak (Matt 5:40) would be to become naked, because most people only owned these two items of clothing.[7] Roman soldiers could force locals to carry their heavy military packs one mile—to offer to go a second mile could be a kind of creative nonviolent resistance (Matt 5:41).

All three of these examples add up to the following: *You wanted to make me feel weak, embarrassed, and angry by dominating me; instead I will surprise you by my creative response in which I take moral control of the situation by refusing to retaliate.* Stassen saw this as the transforming initiative, and he did not get there first. This was how both Mohandas Gandhi and Martin Luther King read the text as well. It became the moral engine of their nonviolent civil disobedience strategies. As both Gandhi and King said: *We will respond to your physical force with our soul force.*

This sets us up for a similar reading of Matt 5:43–48. The traditional teaching is rendered as "you shall love your neighbor and hate your enemy" (Matt 5:43). There wasn't a biblical text that said precisely this—but it is implicit in various places in the OT, and it is certainly structured into "natural" human relations everywhere. We are good and they are bad, we are to take care of each other, and they are to be scorned and destroyed. This is another example where it is the traditional teaching/universal understanding that itself constitutes the sinful pattern that must be overcome for God's will to prevail.

The transforming initiative is found in Matt 5:44, with the rest serving as explanation. The imperatives are to "love your enemies and pray for those who persecute you." The exhortation to pray helps more than it might seem: to "love" an enemy seems both inexhaustible and impossible, but to pray for an enemy, while difficult, is within reach. Even if what we pray is to ask God that the enemy might stop doing harmful things to us, we are still bringing them before God.

The supporting explanations Jesus offers are that loving enemies is a) how we become or demonstrate that we are "children of [God the] Father in heaven" (Matt 5:45), b) God cares for both the evil and the good daily (Matt 5:45), and c) even tax collectors and gentiles treat their kin and loved ones kindly (Matt 5:46–47), and surely we want to do better than that, and

---

7. Davies/Allison Jr., *Matthew*, 546, note that Jesus nonviolently suffered both such slaps and the taking of his clothes.

finally d) The goal is to be "perfect" (Matt 5:48)—perhaps better rendered *complete*—completely loving—as God is.[8]

These teachings make perfect sense and yet seem perfectly impossible—at least in some moods and in relation to some people. There are good reasons why for two millennia Christian heads have snapped back hard at the force of these exhortations to nonretaliation and enemy love.

Yes, it does seem perfectly impossible to go against our every self-protective instinct. And no, however much we might want to resemble God our Father, we are definitely not perfect like God. That sure sounds like radical perfectionism and impossible high ideals. Culpepper writes, "Jesus offers practical examples of a wholly impractical way of life."[9] But does that really capture what Jesus is teaching here?

Because it *is* true that daily God does send sun and rain on the earth, which bring life both to enemies and friends of God. Murderers do receive the gift of beating hearts, vicious people are blessed with beautiful sunsets, and bullies experience love. And, yes, the Creator God does treat humans with care regardless of how they act. Also, Jesus promises there will be a judgment where people face accountability (cf. Matt 25:31–46, Luke 16:19–31), and we take comfort in that.[10]

But more than that, we can see that Jesus is trying to bring into existence a community in which people are "pure in heart" (Matt 5:8), single-minded, radically God-centered and God-imitating and God-obeying. Not human like ordinary run-of-the-mill humanity, but more like the God of the universe who offers love even to those who respond with indifference, scorn, or evil. To be like this God is to move toward nonretaliation and enemy love. It is to refuse to allow the behavior of others to hinder the neighbor-love to which we are committed.

Jesus says that it is God rather than people who sets the agenda for how God will relate to people, and God's agenda is love. He is inviting us to enter this sublime freedom of love, rather than allowing the worst actions of others to entice the worst in us.

---

8. Culpepper, *Matthew*, 120–21, considers a range of translations including perfect, whole, blameless, fully developed in a moral sense, or even as the promise or prediction of perfection.

9. Culpepper, *Matthew*, 118.

10. Davies/Allison Jr., *Matthew*, 540, emphasize that, for Jesus, "The law of reciprocity is not utterly repudiated but only taken out of human hands."

Yes, it's hard. To be like God rather than to do what comes naturally or what everyone else does is hard. But that is the invitation Jesus is offering to his kingdom-of-God community. And it is not impossible.

It does help to notice that Jesus is calling us to actions, not feelings. He's not asking us to feel affection toward those who have wronged us. He's asking us to refrain from retaliation—and to attempt transforming initiatives to defuse conflict. He's asking us to pray for an enemy rather than to wish ill on them.

Enemy-hood works through the natural logic of retaliation in kind.

Enemy-love works through the unnatural divine logic of grace.

Enemy-hood robs us of the freedom to choose our own moral actions.

Enemy-love makes us free again.

Enemy-hood means being overcome by evil.

Enemy-love means overcoming evil with good (Rom 12:21).

People who are determined to love their enemies are the freest and, in some ways, the most powerful people in the world. They set their own agenda, and no one can distract them from it. Thurman points out what a hard inner journey it is to get there—a journey through fear, through anger, even through hate, all the way to love.[11] But when you do get there, it is sublime.

This freedom, this power, this love, is what we see when we look at Jesus himself. He did what he taught. That radical integrity should be our aspiration.

11. Thurman, *Jesus and the Disinherited*, chs. 2, 4, 5.

16

Practicing Piety Privately

But whenever you pray, go into your room and shut the door and pray to your Father who is in secret, and your Father who sees in secret will reward you.

—*MATT 6:6*

Pray, then, in this way:

Our Father in heaven,
may your name be revered as holy.

May your kingdom come.
May your will be done
on earth as it is in heaven.

—*MATT 6:9–10*

Texts: Matt 6:1–18/Luke 11:1–13, cf. Matt 7:7–11

THE LORD'S PRAYER IS one of the handful of Bible passages that made the leap from Scripture to an enduring place in Christian liturgy and private prayer. There are very few other biblical texts that could meet that description.

It seems likely that Jesus did teach his followers some version of this simple prayer, and it remained part of the practice of the earliest Christians after his death and resurrection. It then made it into two of the four Gospel accounts, written decades later, and it continues to be prayed today. The Lord's Prayer is precious to believers at an emotional level because of its message, its simplicity, and its connection to Jesus.[1]

It is interesting as we look at Matthew and Luke side by side to see that both introduce the Lord's Prayer, but that they do it in two different ways.

Luke has Jesus praying off by himself, as he often did. Then his disciples ask him to teach them to pray. Jesus introduces a very simple version of the prayer—so simple that later NT manuscripts felt the need to amend and expand it:

> Father, may your name be revered as holy.
> May your kingdom come.
> Give us each day our daily bread.
> And forgive us our sins,
> for we ourselves forgive everyone indebted to us.
> And do not bring us to the time of trial. (Luke 11:2–4)

Luke then goes on to record Jesus encouraging his disciples to demonstrate persistence and confidence in prayer, using examples from everyday life.

The first example (Luke 11:5–8) suggests that praying is like knocking on the door of a friend's house at midnight when you need some food to offer guests who have arrived unexpectedly. In this situation, eventually, your friend will open the door and get you the food. (This example assumes a sense of community and the utter obligation of offering hospitality that many cultures no longer retain.)

The second example (Luke 11:11–12/Matt 7:9–11) compares praying to a child asking a parent for some food to eat. The parent will naturally give the child an egg or a fish rather than a scorpion or a snake. The payoff line is

---

1. Culpepper, *Matthew*, 128, says this of the composition of the Lord's Prayer: "Clearly, the Lord's Prayer as we know it is the final result of a process of liturgical use and editing . . . While the evidence of multistage composition gives pause to those intent on identifying the words of Jesus, the editorial activity testifies to the importance of the prayer in the early church." Culpepper also notes that ancient tradition gives us three very similar versions of the Lord's Prayer: Matt 6:9–13, Luke 11:2–4, and the Didache 8:2, the latter a very early Christian teaching document. Culpepper, *Matthew*, 127.

deceptively simple: "If you then, who are evil, know how to give good gifts to your children, how much more will the heavenly Father give . . ."[2]

Matthew includes that kind of exhortation near the end of the SM (Matt 7:7–11). But in Matt 6:1–18, the Evangelist weaves the Lord's Prayer into the middle of a teaching on hidden piety. In doing so he makes it part of a moral teaching. That teaching is that disciples should practice their acts of piety, such as giving alms, praying, and fasting, privately rather than publicly. The reason is because doing religious acts in public to receive the positive recognition of others is a corruption of their purpose.

"Beware of practicing your righteousness before others in order to be seen by them, for then you have no reward from your Father in heaven" (Matt 6:1).

This is not a teaching of moral perfectionism, though it is incredibly shrewd in its understanding of human nature, including religious folks' human nature. As social creatures, we are embedded in communities. In those communities we like to be seen as good and praised by others. We like other people to admire us. We like to be noticed and receive praise.

When this dynamic unfolds in a religious context it is even more heightened because the praise we are getting is supposedly for our piety before God. People are looking at us and telling us how devout and good we are. This combination of honor and piety is an intoxicant, which, Jesus teaches, moves us away from God in the name of God.

In *Kingdom Ethics*, we treat this threefold teaching in Matt 6:1–18 in the triadic formula.[3]

Traditional Righteousness: Give alms, pray, and fast.

Robert Gundry claims that these are "the three main pillars of Jewish piety,"[4] deeply embedded in the Jewish tradition. Regular prayer and periodic fasting are obviously taught in the Hebrew Bible. Care for the poor is also a major theme (cf. Deut 15:11), and "almsgiving" was especially emphasized in later sacred literature such as Sirach (Sir 3:30, 7:10, 12:3, 16:14) and Tobit (Tob 4:6–11, 12:8–9, 14:2, 14:9–11) that did not make it into the Protestant Bible. Jesus does not abrogate these teachings on almsgiving, prayer, and fasting, but instead affirms them.

Sinful Pattern: Giving alms, praying, and fasting "in order to be seen."

---

2. This is a *qal vahomer* move—an argument from lesser to greater, using "how much more" to get there.

3. Gushee/Stassen, *Kingdom Ethics*, ch. 17, cf. 340–343.

4. Robert Gundry, quoted in Gushee/Stassen, *Kingdom Ethics*, 340.

This is a sinful pattern because acts of piety are supposed to be offered to God out of devotion of heart and obedience, not offered around other people for their attention. "The pride of show is a malignant growth on religion which leads to counterfeit goodness."[5] This connects to the Beatitude where Jesus says, "Blessed are the pure in heart" (Matt 5:8). If we are aiming acts of piety *both* at God and at people, we are double-minded; we are not demonstrating that singleness of purpose that was so important to Jesus. The consequence: "Those who practice their piety to be seen by others have received all the reward they will ever see."[6]

Transforming Initiative: Do your acts of piety privately.

This is a transforming initiative because it is impossible to be praised by other people for something if they have no idea that you are doing it. Give anonymously. Pray at home. Fast without drawing attention to yourself.

These are the two different ways that Luke and Matthew situate the Lord's Prayer. Both make sense. Together they enrich our contextualization of that prayer.

When we compare Matthew's and Luke's Lord's Prayer, we can see that Matthew employs a slightly expanded version.

The petitions are so lovely, so simple.[7]

We are to pray to God our Father that God's Name be revered (hallowed, honored).[8] Our first petition is for God to be honored appropriately (Matt 6:9). We seek not our own praise, not our own honor, but God's.

Then we are to ask for the kingdom of God to come (Matt 6:10).[9] In Matthew, Jesus adds some crucial Hebrew parallelism, essentially defining the kingdom as "your will be done on earth as it is in heaven." Note the built-in tension between God bringing the kingdom and humans choosing

5. Davies/Allison Jr., *Matthew*, 576.

6. Gushee/Stassen, *Kingdom Ethics*, 341. Michael Joseph Brown, "Gospel of Matthew," in Blount, *True to Our Native Land*, 92, adds: "It means 'paid in full' . . . To put it another way, if one can only be punished once for a bad deed, then one can only be rewarded once for a good one."

7. Gushee/Stassen, *Kingdom Ethics*, 353–55 offers a longer exposition.

8. Amy Jill-Levine, "Gospel of Matthew," in *Women's Bible Commentary*, 470, notes the difficulty of father language "for readers who suffered abuse at the hands of their fathers or who chafe at patriarchal language. Perhaps, however, the address 'father' can function to show the beneficent role fathers in antiquity did play." She also suggests that the phrase "may have political resonances," demoting any human authority, such as the Roman emperor, from claiming divine fatherhood status.

9. Culpepper, *Matthew*, 130, shows that the petitions call for God's response, thus a translation like "Let your kingdom come" (or "bring your kingdom rule") is better.

to do God's will, which is constitutive of the kingdom.[10] Prayer trains our desires—praying for the kingdom is to be trained away from pursuing our own kingdoms, and thus to ready ourselves to be a part of God's kingdom.

We then ask for "daily bread" (Matt 6:11)—sufficient food—signaling the precarious economic position of most of Jesus' listeners, and setting a moral baseline. People need food enough for the day—not less, but also not more. People who do not know whether they will have daily bread have deeply identified with—and often prayed—this prayer.

We ask for (debt) forgiveness (Matt 6:12), tied to our willingness to be forgiving of others.[11] This will be the subject of our next chapter.

We ask to be spared trials (Matt 6:13) or temptations (either term is a legitimate translation), whether believed to be sent by God or Satan or life,[12] with Matthew adding a prayer for rescue from evil, or the evil one. Trials come, from whatever source; we ask that we not be overcome by them.

Those who pray as Jesus taught are first oriented toward the honoring of God's name and the advance of God's reign. We ask for sufficient food to live, for us and for all. We are reminded of the centrality of forgiveness both from God and toward others. We are aware of our vulnerability as sinners, and we ask to be spared trials and temptations too great for us.

There is a good reason we come back to the Lord's Prayer, again and again. It is a crucial part of the theological, spiritual, and moral teaching of Jesus.

10. Culpepper, *Matthew*, 131.

11. Varying renderings of the Lord's Prayer even today vacillate between "forgive us our debts" and "forgive us our trespasses/sins." Culpepper, *Matthew*, 126, 133, argues that "debts" is the better translation, and of course using that term opens up the massive problem of debt, and the need for debt forgiveness, both in Jesus' world and in our own.

12. Culpepper, *Matthew*, 136, explores the difficult challenge of interpreting this brief petition, which he concludes has the sense of "voic[ing] trust in God's sovereignty" amid the trials (external testing) and temptations (internal testing) that will continue until the kingdom comes in its fullness.

17

Forgiving

For if you forgive others their trespasses, your heavenly Father will also forgive you, but if you do not forgive others, neither will your Father forgive your trespasses.

—MATT 6:14–15

Texts: Matt 6:14–15, cf. 18:10–35, Mark 11:25–26, Luke 17:3–4

IT IS MATTHEW WHO has the most expansive treatment of Jesus' teaching about forgiveness, though the issue is also addressed in Mark and Luke. As we have just seen, it is woven into the centrally important Lord's Prayer (Matt 6:14–15). It receives extended treatment in Matt 18:10–35. There Jesus teaches both a process of confronting sin in the church, and the centrality of forgiveness.

In Mark 11:25, Jesus teaches his listeners to forgive, "whenever you stand praying . . . if you have anything against anyone." This makes forgiveness a central aspect of *everyday* prayer. It implicitly encourages those who pray to include honest awareness of wounds received, grudges held, "anything against anyone," and then to forgive these as part of the act of praying.

There are five Greek words that we see translated to some form of the English "forgive" that are used in the New Testament:

- *aphesis*—This word appears seventeen times in the NT and is often translated as "forgiveness" or "remission." It is a noun that can also be translated as "release" or "freedom."

- *charis*—This word appears over 150 times in the NT and is most commonly translated as "grace." However, it can also be translated as "forgiveness," "favor," or "kindness."

- *hileōs*—This word is interesting because it appears only once in the NT in Heb 2:17 and is translated as "merciful" or "propitiation." However, it is closely related to the verb *hilaskomai,* which means "to propitiate" or "to make atonement."

- *suggnōme*—This word appears twice in the NT in 2 Cor 2:7–8 and is translated as "forgiveness" or "pardon." It can also be translated as "indulgence" or "forbearance." The connotation of these English words suggests that this one is specifically about forgiving someone who deserves to be punished.

- *aphiēmi*—This word appears over 140 times in the NT and is most commonly translated as "to leave" or "to let go." But in some contexts, it can be "to forgive" or "to pardon." It is the word used in all the texts we are considering here.

Jesus routinely appears to make God's forgiveness of us contingent on our forgiveness of others. The logic is "if, then": if you forgive others, God will forgive you. But also, there is the corollary: if you don't forgive others, God will not forgive you. Davies and Allison write: "By placing the negatives . . . after the positives . . . the evangelist shows that for him the stress lies on the warning of judgement rather than on the promise of forgiveness."[1]

This ought to make anyone the least bit aware of their own offenses against God feel deeply humbled and even frightened. Humbled about the wrongs we have committed in God's sight, for God sees all; frightened of God's negative judgment on us. But the good news is that if we can become people of mercy and forgiveness toward those that offend us, God will be moved to mercy and forgiveness toward us. That is what Jesus is teaching.

Jesus just assumes that in human life people offend and hurt each other and end up with grievances held tightly in their hearts. Who can challenge this assumption? It is just a fact, sad but undeniable. Still, it is meaningful that Jesus understands it. The question he is raising is not whether we or

1. Davies/Allison Jr., *Matthew,* 616.

those around us will live such a perfect life that we never offend or are offended; the real question is whether we will freely open our hearts in forgiveness when we have been offended. This is such a routine problem in human life that daily prayer appears to be the setting in which we are to take daily inventory and daily offer forgiveness!

This also suggests a certain reading of the character of God and how God looks upon us. We are loved, we are understood, we are forgiven, and we are called to higher ground.

We are *loved*—God made us and loves us and dignifies us with his care and attention.

We are *understood* for the fractured, fractious mess that we are, individually and collectively.

We are *forgiven* of our sins; God decides not to hold our sins against us.

We are *called to higher ground* through the demanding but realistic command to forgive daily those who wound us. Higher ground here is not a perfect record in avoiding giving or receiving offense, but instead a commitment to forgive (and for that matter, to accept forgiveness).

That ties in nicely with the Lord's Prayer. The request "forgive us our debts, as we also have forgiven our debtors," appears right after "give us this day our daily bread" (Matt 6:12, 11). Forgiveness is like daily bread. We need to offer it, and we need to receive it. Matthew's Jesus then adds a corollary at the end of the Lord's Prayer. It expands Mark's teaching a bit and makes the conditionality of God's forgiveness painfully clear: if you forgive, God will forgive you; if not, not. "The community of Jesus' followers must be one in which prayers for forgiveness are supported by the practice of forgiving."[2]

Matt 18 offers a rather grand and detailed expansion of Jesus' teaching on forgiveness. Matthew seems to be doing some pastoral legislating for his church community.

In Matt 18:10–14 he takes the image of the lost sheep as a setup for his teaching on conflict and forgiveness in the church. Now the lost sheep appears to be the church member who has sinned (Matt 18:15) and has therefore gone astray like a lost sheep. Note that this reads like a teaching on forgiveness if "sins *against you*" is the reading of Matt 18:15; but some Greek manuscripts lack the "against you."

A careful, step-by-step process is then described for "regaining" that brother or sister. It involves candidly pointing out the sin of the other, first by one, then by a handful, and finally by the whole church, all in an effort to

---

2. Culpepper, *Matthew*, 137.

bring the straying sheep back into the fold. This is a church discipline process, a delicate and demanding effort. Sometimes this effort fails, and this process has been abandoned in most parts of the contemporary church.

It is only in Matt 18:21 that the interpersonal forgiveness process is clearly the focus. This begins when Peter asks Jesus how many times he must forgive a brother or sister who has sinned against him. Peter ventures an estimate of seven times.[3] Jesus' response is a dramatic expansion—seventy-seven times, or 70 x 7 = 490 times, which is almost like saying there is no limit on how many times we should forgive.

Jesus then illustrates his teaching with the dramatic parable of the unforgiving servant, who, though he has been shown extraordinary mercy by his master related to a massive debt, does not similarly forgive someone who owes *him* far less. His master finds out, revokes his forgiveness, and punishes him severely. Jesus then says, "so my heavenly Father will also do to every one of you if you do not forgive your brother or sister from your heart" (Matt 18:35). It almost appears that an unforgivable sin in God's sight is unforgiveness.

Certainly, Jesus makes the demand to forgive very clear. It is an essential aspect of being Christ's people. As Davies and Allison put it: "the right of the eschatological community to utter the Lord's Prayer depends, as does the efficacy of the prayer, upon communal reconciliation . . . [it] must be prayed by a church whose members have forgiven one another."[4]

When one thinks of the deep divisions, the casually broken relationships, and the bitter unforgiveness that so often characterizes the contemporary churches, our manifest disobedience is hard to deny.

There are all kinds of details and issues that a deep dive into forgiveness raises, such as whether forgiveness always requires remaining in relationship, or whether we must forgive even when the other person is not sorry or is continuing to harm us (compare Matt 18 with Luke 17:3–4!). I have dealt with these issues at length elsewhere.[5]

For now, we leave it here, with this gracious yet demanding moral teaching of Jesus: that those who would please God do not seem to be expected to live sinless, conflict-free lives in this sinful, fractured world. But

---

3. JANT, 45, cites a rabbinic source that says one is only required to seek forgiveness three times, though the Jewish sources also urge a readiness to forgive and tie God's willingness to forgive us with our willingness to forgive others.

4. Davies/Allison Jr., *Matthew*, 617.

5. Gushee, *Introducing Christian Ethics*, ch. 12.

we *are* expected amid this sinfulness to offer the daily spiritual bread of forgiveness. When we are hurt and angry this is the one option available to us that pleases God. The only alternative is hardness of heart, grudge-holding, and permanent breaches in our relationships, both with neighbor and with God.

18

Storing up Treasure in Heaven

Do not store up for yourselves treasures on earth, where moth and rust consume and where thieves break in and steal, but store up for yourselves treasures in heaven . . . For where your treasure is, there your heart will be also.

—MATT 6:19–21

Texts: Matt 6:19–34/Luke 11:34–36, cf. Luke 12:22–34

MATTHEW HAS ASSEMBLED SEVERAL memorable Jesus-sayings about material things into one powerful, compelling, and demanding section, which we consider here. Together they leave quite an impression, the implications of which Christians have been contemplating, evading, debating, and (rarely) practicing for two millennia.[1]

The four core sayings passed on by the oral tradition add up to what I have outlined below. They do not appear in John and only in one phrase in Mark. Matthew puts them all here in chapter 6, while Luke scatters them a bit. The parallels look like this:

---

1. Gushee/Stassen, *Kingdom Ethics*, ch. 18, treats economic ethics with a focus on these texts.

- Store up treasures in heaven rather than on earth. Where your treasure is, your heart also will be (Matt 6:19–21/Luke 12:33–34; cf. Mark 10:21).

- The eye is the lamp of the body (Matt 6:22–23/Luke 11:34–36).

- No one can serve two masters. You cannot serve both God and Mammon (Matt 6:24/Luke 16:13).

- Do not worry about your life, what you will eat or drink (Matt 6:25–34/Luke 12:22–32).

When one considers these four sayings, especially as further elaborated in these texts, and then ponders well other sayings of Jesus about material life, a pattern emerges that is hard to deny. What we supposed followers of Jesus do with it is up to us, but the pattern is present.

Jesus teaches that God the loving heavenly Parent knows about the material needs of all the creatures (animal and human) that have been created, and God provides for us like all good parents provide for their children. We can therefore ask God, and trust God, for the needed basics, such as food, drink, and clothing, and stop worrying about how we will acquire what we need.

Plus, Jesus reminds us, worrying is fruitless anyway. The significance to God of our basic material needs is clear when Jesus teaches us to pray for daily bread, which can stand in for other daily material needs as well. People (and animals) need to be fed, housed, and warmed against the cold. God knows this, and in love God provides.

From this posture of trust, we can see the world properly and not develop a dark, unhealthy, or evil eye, metaphors for covetousness, stinginess, and greed, which at their core flow out of looking at the world in fear of not having enough.[2] This fearfulness can flower into all kinds of evils, including hyper-competitiveness in the economic sphere, economic exploitation of others, indifference to the poor and needy, and a fixation on the acquisition of material things ("storing up treasures on earth") in a vain attempt to ensure our own security in a world that cannot be trusted.

---

2. Davies/Allison Jr., *Matthew*, 635–39, show both that the text reveals a premodern understanding of how vision works, but that its deeper meaning is as a spiritual-ethical truth long recognized in the Jewish tradition with the language of the good eye and the evil eye: "one's moral disposition correlates with a religious state, with the darkness or light within" (639). I might also add the observation that the look in a person's eyes does sometimes seem to reveal something about the darkness or light within them, and about how they "look" at the world.

Jesus uses the Aramaic word *mamona* (Mammon, in most English translations) to describe not just wealth but the turning of wealth into an idol that displaces God in the human heart. This idol affects human choices—and invites God's wrath. Anything that we trust, serve, pursue, long for, and (in effect) worship can become a competing god to the one true God. The ban on idolatry is the very first of the Ten Commandments, and it permeates Jesus' teaching as well.

The original meaning of the Aramaic term *mamona* was "trust," or "reliance."[3] It is as if the concepts of trust and wealth had simply merged linguistically as they do so often in reality. Jesus identifies wealth, money, material goods, and a life consumed by the greedy quest for such, as an idol. This helps make sense of his call both in Luke 12:32 and in other places for some or all his followers to sell all their possessions. It is hard to make an idol out of something that one has abandoned.

It has been interesting for me to meet Christians who have attempted radical divestment of their property as Jesus taught. They testify that it is not so much the material uses of their former possessions that they miss, but the identity-forming and social status roles they once played. They miss not just a car to get around in, but the BMW that signaled their earning power.

Even way back then, long before the development of rapacious modern consumer capitalism, Jesus saw the systemic nature of greed. Mammon is not just something that arises spontaneously in the solitary human heart, but instead is encouraged in the ethos and structures of economic life and human culture. When status is associated with wealth—and especially when religious folks associate God's blessing and people's virtue with wealth—entire cultures train people into a life of economic anxiety, striving, and exploitation. If storing up treasures on earth is everything, why scruple about whether workers are treated fairly? Or even bother with whether people are paid at all if we can enslave them instead, and make more money in the bargain?

But what if, on the other hand, one rejects the whole Mammon project? This is what Jesus did in his own lifestyle, and it is what Jesus teaches. Cleansing the eye of covetousness and fear, cleansing the heart of anxiety and greed, cleansing the behavior of stinginess, exploitation, and indifference to the poor, the disciple's relationship with the material world and economic culture can be transformed.

3. Gale, in JANT, 24.

We ask from God just enough to care for our needs, sure; but our real project in life is seeking the kingdom of God (Matt 6:33) and thus we are busy storing up treasures in heaven rather than on earth. If we have more than we need, we respond with grateful sharing with those who have less.[4] We are always attentive to the poor and ready to give alms (Matt 6:2). We are even open to selling what we have and moving into an even more radical place of trust, because our life is governed and ensured by God, not by Mammon.[5]

Our relationship to the material world, and thus to our neighbors, is transformed. We are the freest of all people, able to look with compassionate love on our neighbors, grateful for the little we have, empowered to move about the world without the maladies of Mammonism distorting our vision and behavior.

Is this a counsel of unreachable moral perfectionism? Many have thought so, and it certainly cannot be described as the characteristic pattern of the Christian middle and upper classes in any era. We (I count myself here) have participated in the normal patterns of economic striving, saving, and securing funds for the future. Jesus' radical path in economic life does not seem to make much sense for the average family trying to meet monthly bills, pay for insurance, and send kids to college.

It is interesting to consider how even someone as morally perfectionist as John Wesley ended up summarizing his economic ethic as *gain all you can, save all you can, and give all you can.*[6] The giving part certainly reflects Jesus' spirit, while the rest of it hardly coheres. This is a bit of Jesus plus an awful lot of early British capitalism and prudential saving for a rainy day. But it is a better economic ethic than that practiced by many Christians today, which looks more like *earn all you can, spend more, borrow much, save little, and hope you die before your 401k runs out.*

Jesus blesses the poor, and the poor come to mind as one seriously considers this teaching. There are billions of people on earth whose choice comes down to anxiety vs. trust amid chronic financial insecurity. These are the many who must worry about whether there will be enough food this

---

4. Culpepper, *Matthew*, 140: "One who . . . gives alms, prays, and fasts—stores up treasure in heaven."

5. Davies/Allison Jr., *Matthew*, 630, write: "The command not to store up treasure on earth should not be understood to entail the renunciation of all possessions." But this was precisely what was required of the man we call the rich young ruler (ch. 9, above). And Luke 12:33 says, "Sell your possession and give alms." A blanket statement of this type is unwarranted. The tension should be retained, the question left open.

6. John Wesley, "Use of Money," in Wogaman, *Readings in Christian Ethics*, 178–81.

week or whether they can pay for health care. They can be consumed, just as anyone else is, by fear and greed.

Or maybe they can choose the radical path of Jesus. Certainly, some of the poorest people I have known are some of the least anxious and most generous. "Blessed are you who are poor, for yours is the kingdom of God" (Luke 6:20). Jesus deeply understood both the great difficulty of the lives of the poor and their perhaps simpler access to spiritual health. Many of the rest of us spend our lives striving to climb up the greasy pole of Mammon to secure those treasures that only last during this lifetime, if they last at all.

19

Judge Not

Do not judge, so that you may not be judged. For the judgment you give will be the judgment you get, and the measure you give will be the measure you get.

—MATT 7:1-2

Texts: Matt 7:1–5/Luke 6:37–42

THERE ARE TEN GREEK words in the NT that can be translated to some form of "judge," "to judge," or "to pass judgement."

Both Matthew and Luke use *krinō*—to judge or decide. *Krinō* occurs 114 times in the NT and is the most straightforward of the terms.

Other options include:

- *dikaiōma*—a judgment or ordinance [four uses = x4]

- *katadikazō*—to condemn or pronounce guilty [x4]

- *katakrinō*—to judge or condemn [x12]

- *anakrinō*—to examine or investigate [x6]

- *dokimazō*—to test or examine [x20]

- *syniēmi*—to understand or perceive [x4]

- *elegchō*—to reprove or rebuke [x17]

- *diakrinō*—to distinguish or discern [x9]

- *paraballō* (parable)—to compare or liken [x1]

The logic of Matt 7:1–5 appears to be as follows: the moral command is "do not judge" other people. This moral command is backed up by a warning of reciprocal judgment—that each of us will be judged by the same standard by which we judge others, "measure for measure."

Most readers probably assume that this is a warning of God's judgment on our harsh and unfair judgments of others, kind of like the warning of God withholding forgiveness based on our unwillingness to forgive those who have wronged us: "you will be judged [by God], and how you respond to others now determines how you are judged in the future."[1]

However, it is also possible to read this more as a wisdom teaching, a "rule of prudence," based on how human relations work.[2] If we are harsh in our judgments of others, that will likely be reciprocated—"the measure you give will be the measure you get." Most of us who have lived awhile can see that this is true.

Probably it is best to see both meanings. The rabbinic sources emphasize fair judgment and warn that we will be judged by others based on how we mete out judgment to them.[3]

The teaching moves on to some brilliant hyperbole about how often we tend to overlook our own large sins while not missing a bit of other people's smaller misdeeds. The idea of somehow being able to see around a log sticking out of our eye to catch a glimpse of the speck in someone else's eye is dead-on accurate while also being laugh-out-loud funny.[4] Jesus goes on to instruct us to "first take the log out of your own eye, and then you will see clearly to take the speck out of your neighbor's eye" (Matt 7:5). The most important moral project for each of us appears to be fixing ourselves, not others. Notice again the use of vision as a metaphor for morality.

Luke's version expands the teaching in Matthew just a bit, adding the harsher word "condemn" (*katadikazō*) to "judge," explicitly connecting both to forgiveness and to generosity, teaching the reciprocity principle in each

1. Culpepper, *Matthew*, 149.

2. Culpepper, *Matthew*, 149.

3. Gale, in JANT, 24.

4. Culpepper, *Matthew*, 150, notes that Jesus, as a carpenter (Matt 13:55), would be quite familiar with the problem of specks of wood in the eyes.

case. The measure for measure image is also enriched beautifully—"Give and it will be given to you. A good measure, pressed down, shaken together, running over, will be put into your lap" (Luke 6:38). This expansion makes clear that the image has to do with receiving a generous measure or portion of something, like flour, in a commercial transaction. If we measure out generously when we are selling, others will measure out generously to us when we are buying. This had more relevance in an era before tight standardization and regulation of commercial weights and measures.

It is a very interesting picture of God that Jesus is offering in this teaching. He depicts a God intimately concerned with the human heart and with the details of how we relate to other people, calibrating the vertical relationship between us and God based on the horizontal relationship between us and others.

Jesus retains a stern picture of a judging God, but then turns it sideways in the direction of mercy. God's harshest, least merciful, and most negative judgments are directed at people who are harsh, unmerciful, and negative in relating to others.

This is very different from a religious spirit in which God's supposed punitiveness is tied to and reinforces human punitiveness. Jesus has a lively doctrine of sin, but the sins he is most concerned about are those that harm others in the name of God, especially those that harm others in the name of God, Law, and Morality. His concern totally comports with the moral emphasis found in the Law and the Prophets.

The practical consequences of this teaching for those seeking to obey Jesus are clear. We are not to posture ourselves as God, standing as Judge over others. We are to relate generously to other people, withholding judgment that is not ours to give. We are to be acutely aware of our own sins and only dimly aware of those of others. We need to remind ourselves that each of us has an audience of One, the only One capable of rendering true judgment. Paul echoes this theme in Rom 14:

> Why do you pass judgment on your brother or sister? Or you, why do you despise your brother or sister? For we will all stand before the judgment seat of God. For it is written,
>
> "As I live, says the Lord, every knee shall bow to me, and every tongue shall give praise to God."
>
> So then, each one of us will be held accountable. (Rom 14:10–12)

"Each one of us will be held accountable"—to God. If we know and believe this, then perhaps we can develop a greater humility in our judgments of others. We remember God is the judge and we are not, and we act accordingly.

Dietrich Bonhoeffer offers a Christ-centered interpretation, emphasizing his consistent theme that followers of Jesus must relate to other people only through Christ:

> Disciples live completely out of the bond connecting them with Jesus Christ. Their righteousness depends only on that bond and never apart from it . . . The disciples' own righteousness is thus hidden from them in their communion with Jesus. They . . . only see Jesus . . . no measuring standard for a righteous life stands between the disciples and other people . . . [they] view other people only as those to whom Jesus comes . . . Jesus' struggle for the other person, his call, his love, his grace, his judgment are all that matters. Thus the disciples do not stand in a position from which the other person is attacked . . . they approach the other person with an unconditional offer of community.[5]

The main idea for Bonhoeffer is that when we look at others, we should see not them but Jesus—what Jesus intends for them, is offering them, is doing in, for, and through them. This makes any posture of judgment difficult.

All of this is very good. The world would be far kinder if this was the approach that characterized most people.

But there is a problem: moral judgments, and indeed legal judgments, often with associated punishments, simply must be made in human life. It is interesting that the rabbinic sources emphasize making *fair* judgments, even *generous* judgments, but not *no* judgments. A posture of complete nonjudgmentalism is radical; indeed, it is probably not workable in any long-term human community.

Human life *just has* a moral structure to it. People routinely think in moral terms—about right and wrong, good and bad, better and worse, virtue and vice.[6] Human communities, beginning with families, depend on most people most of the time doing the right thing. Even the most basic moral codes judge certain acts as right, or as wrong.

---

5. Bonhoeffer, *Discipleship*, 170.

6. Gushee, *Introducing Christian Ethics*, 4, calls this the "intrinsic moral dimension of human experience."

Look at the Ten Commandments. Torah prescribes various negative sanctions to be enforced in the covenant community for violating God's Law. Parents make "laws" for their children and enforce negative judgments on violations. All legal codes do something similar; judges every day send people to prison for violating laws. The reason why people make negative moral judgments about the behavior of others is because morality matters—because behavior matters—because people get hurt by the misdeeds of others toward them.

Surely Jesus cannot be saying that all this moral structure in God's world and in human community is just to be set aside as we take a posture of complete nonjudgmentalism. As Davies and Allison put it: "The imperative . . . cannot refer to simple ethical judgements, and believers are not being instructed to refrain from critical thinking."[7]

Remember, Jesus explicitly stated that he did not come to abolish the Law (Matt 5:17–20). Yet that is sometimes how this passage is read, often with morally confused effects, in which people feel they can never make even the most obvious negative moral judgment on any behavior. This misinterpretation has contributed to an encroaching moral relativism in Christian circles. How many times have we heard someone say "Don't judge me," or "Who am I to judge?" in situations in which a moral judgment is demanded?

Can it be that Jesus' radicalism, his radical Godwardness, is indeed so radical, that the moral judgments that make everyday community possible simply do not matter to him? I don't think so.

Perhaps our best reading is the following: even while we must make human moral judgments—as parents, teachers, governors, judges, citizens, church members, fellow humans—we must do so in a spirit of generosity, mercy, and humility, always remembering that moral scrutiny begins with ourselves, and that the ultimate judgment on a human life belongs to God alone. While we might be required to judge certain acts as right or wrong, "we are to confine ourselves to that field and refrain from passing judgement on persons."[8]

7. Davies/Allison Jr., *Matthew*, 668.
8. Davies/Allison Jr., *Matthew*, 669, quoting T. W. Manson.

20

The Golden Rule

In everything do to others as you would have them do to you, for this is the Law and the Prophets.

—*MATT 7:12*

Texts: Matt 7:12/Luke 6:31

EMBEDDED INCONSPICUOUSLY NEAR THE tail end of the Sermon on the Mount is a saying of Jesus that some consider not just the high point of Jesus' teaching, but the most important moral exhortation ever uttered on earth.[1] This statement, which for centuries has been called "the Golden Rule," remains familiar even in post-Christian cultures. The difficulty in wanting to obey this demanding rule is signified by the cynical variations one sometimes hears, like: *Do unto others before they do unto you.*

One reason why the Golden Rule is unforgettable is because of its simplicity. Treat others how you would want to be treated.[2] A four-year-old

---

1. Davies/Allison Jr., *Matthew*, 686, claim that this statement is "not only the quintessence of the law and the prophets but also the quintessence of the sermon on the mount and thus the quintessence of Jesus' teaching."

2. Culpepper, *Matthew*, 153, calls attention to the universality of "others." No limits are accepted.

can understand this teaching. It is just as simple whether framed positively or negatively:

As you would want someone to treat you, treat them that way.

If you would not want someone to treat you that way, don't treat them that way.[3]

This teaching could be described in terms of fairness. It is only fair that the same standard of behavior should be applied to me as it is to you, and to you as it is to me. It has obvious applications to numerous arenas of life. It works just as well in relationships of equal power as unequal power.

In a relationship of equal power: I should treat my friend with the consideration that I would want my friend to offer me.

In a relationship of unequal power: A boss should treat an employee the way the boss would wish to be treated if she were the employee in a different place and time.

The Golden Rule has applications to governmental and institutional contexts. Here is an example:

After the 9/11 attacks, the US government authorized the brutal mistreatment of some of the suspected terrorists held in US custody. I got involved in the public resistance to this mistaken policy change. One of the arguments that gained traction for those trying to resist this abuse was this simple application of the Golden Rule: *The US military should treat foreign nationals that we are detaining the way that we would want our people treated by the military forces of other countries.*

It is important to differentiate the Golden Rule from the principle of reciprocity that was so omnipresent in the world that Jesus inhabited, and not unfamiliar in our own world. That principle went something like this:

Do good unto others today *so that* they will do good unto you tomorrow.

We invite you to our lavish party today, so that you will invite us to your lavish party next week.

I help on your bank heist tonight, so that you help on my grand theft auto tomorrow night.

I vote for your bill in Congress today, so that you vote for mine tomorrow.

3. Culpepper, *Matthew*, 153, notes negatively stated versions of this norm going back to Herodotus and appearing in the intertestamental literature (Tob 4:15) and in the Talmud, but he claims that Jesus offers the first known positive formulation. In ethics, positive obligations (here is what you must do) are more demanding than negative ones (here is what you must not do), because they are more open-ended.

With all three examples, this is just the old principle of "you scratch my back, I scratch yours." It is reciprocal dealmaking for the purpose of self-interest. There is nothing *moral* about it. One can hear Jesus saying, "even the tax collectors and Gentiles do the same" (cf. Matt 5:46–47).

Jesus is teaching something different. His rule is not about worldly reciprocity but about establishing for oneself a pattern of behavior ahead of *and unrelated to* the behavior of others. Act toward others today the way that you *would want them* to act toward you tomorrow.

The implicit follow-on phrase would be, "even if they do not act that way toward you tomorrow." That's because the principle of treating others as you would want to be treated does not depend on the actual behavior of the others you encounter. If our actions are instead based on a principle more like *do to others what they have already done to you*, that returns us to *lex talionis*, to an eye for an eye. Jesus has already made it abundantly clear that he is teaching a higher righteousness than that.

Jesus wants to train people—not just individuals but a kingdom-of-God community—to let God's will rather than mere human reactivity set the agenda for their behavior. If *the other*, especially an oppressive other, determines how we act, then we are the unhappiest of people. That's because not only are we being harmed by the other person, but we are also allowing that miserable oppressor to determine *our* actions.

True spiritual freedom, as pastor-theologian Howard Thurman understood, involves wrestling back inner control of our motivations and accepting divine direction of our behavior.[4] Thus: I will do to you as I would want to be done by, regardless, because it is God's will that sets my agenda and God's Spirit who governs my actions, and no one can take that away from me.

Consider this as a vision for the Christian church, not just in our internal church relations, but also in our engagement with the outside world. Knowing that the Golden Rule, according to Jesus, summarizes the entire content of the Law and the Prophets—and therefore of God's will—we seek to act toward others as we wish they would act toward us, regardless of how they do act toward us. Here would be a community of human beings within which the power of merely negative reactivity is at last broken. That would make the church the community of the freest people on the planet. That kind of community would indeed bring glory to God and hope to the world.

---

4. Thurman, *Jesus and the Disinherited*, 98–99. Ultimately, this is the theme of the whole book.

21

Fruit, Deeds, and Houses Built on Rock

You will know them by their fruits . . . every good tree bears good fruit, but the bad tree bears bad fruit. A good tree cannot bear bad fruit, nor can a bad tree bear good fruit.

—*MATT 7:16–A, 17–18*

Not everyone who says to me, "Lord, Lord," will enter the kingdom of heaven, but only the one who does the will of my Father in heaven.

—*Matt 7:21*

Everyone, then, who hears these words of mine and acts on them will be like a wise man who built his house on rock.

—*MATT 7:24*

Texts: Matt 7:13–29/Luke 6:43–49, cf. Matt 12:33–37

IN THE CLOSING WORDS of the Sermon on the Mount, Jesus offers one final teaching, emphasizing that *what God cares about is our action in obedience to God's will, which is the truest revelation of the state of our heart.*

Jesus begins with the dire warning that "the gate is narrow and the road is hard that leads to life, and there are few who find it" (Matt 7:13–15).

This should not surprise us by now. For eleven chapters we have been considering the SM. Jesus certainly does offer radical instruction in God's will. While I have argued that he does not teach mere aspirations or gauzy impossibilities, his teachings are demanding. Even the triadic, transforming initiatives interpretation, where it applies, still asks disciples to do hard things. It is striking that as he ends this sermon, Jesus is already conceding that "few" will take the path he has illuminated.

But many will claim to do so. There are many false prophets (Matt 7:15). To determine who is a "wolf in sheep's clothing" takes discernment. But there is one clear test: "You will know them by their fruits" (Matt 7:16).

There is OT background (1 Sam 24:13, Prov 11:30) for this image of "fruit." Luke uses it in his parallel Sermon on the Plain, while Matthew deploys it separately in 12:33–35. The parallels take the metaphor into more detail and precision: the heart is the source of a person's words and deeds—whatever is contained therein, whether good or evil, is ultimately revealed in the "fruit" of that person's life. A person with a good heart is like a good tree bearing good fruit; the reverse is, sadly, also true. The state of a person's heart becomes, let us say, constitutional—people are what they are, in their core, their heart—and they bear the fruits reflecting who they are. Here in Matthew 7:19 Jesus offers the warning that bad trees (people) bearing bad fruit (wrong actions) face the fire of judgment, just as unfruitful fruit trees will be cut down and burned.

In terms of moral teaching, this image has been a powerful and influential one. It has been taken as a major statement related to what has been called character ethics, which emphasizes the inner moral self that people develop and that shapes their lives. Jesus offers enough here to give us a basic theory of character: there is a "heart," an inner moral core, in every person. It is formed, at least in part, by what we treasure. Out of this heart, this moral core, flow human actions, notably words and deeds. Actions flow from character and can be called the "fruits" of a person's life. They tend to be consistent with character and can be generally characterized as good or bad. The one who sets that standard, who determines what good fruit and bad fruit look like, is God, and in the end, God will render judgment on the fruit of each human life.

There are so many implications here. Among them is the centrality of character and its development. Jesus seems to be saying that we do (action) what we are (character). Our "fruit" reflects the overall health of the "tree" that is the moral self. Thus, all who care about how people act should care about character development. This has major implications for parents, educators, criminal justice officials, and religious leaders—really for anyone who cares about what kinds of people end up living in our communities.

But there is an ongoing cyclical relationship between character and action, heart and fruit, that Jesus doesn't quite develop here. Just as character drives action, action forms character. A major factor in how we become good or bad in our heart is our own actions. For example, if we routinely choose to resort to physical violence, then our hearts become more violent.

So, the tree/fruit, or character/action dynamic may be more cyclical, more cumulative. Shaped early in a certain direction by our childhood and temperament, we then use our ever-increasing youth-to-adult freedom to make certain choices, which either reshape our character or, more likely, reinforce its built-in tendencies. "What one is is what one does: the deeds are the man."[1] We are not enslaved by the early character formation that we experienced, but we are affected by it. Still, God holds us accountable for our lives and choices.

Ultimately, that is the major implication not only of the tree/fruit metaphor, but also the rest of the passage. It is action that matters to God.

Not everyone who calls out the name of the Lord enters the kingdom of heaven. Not everyone who has identified the right God by the right name. Not everyone who prophesies in the name of Jesus. Not everyone who casts out demons or does other miracles. The one who pleases God is the one who does God's will, defined here as hearing and acting on Jesus' words. No religious activity or profession matters, relative to that test. This is my rather literal restatement of Matt 7:21–23.[2]

Given that this unique teaching (not found elsewhere in the Gospels) is placed here at the end of the SM, it ought to inspire a retrospective look at everything he has just been teaching. Jesus, like Moses, goes up on the mountain and teaches his followers to defuse conflict by making peace, avoid adultery, keep marriage covenants, turn the other cheek, love enemies, not practice piety for show, live in simplicity, trust God, reject greed, not judge others, and do to others as we would be done by.

1. Davies/Allison Jr., *Matthew*, 709.

2. Culpepper, *Matthew*, 158, rightly identifies the significance of this passage for considering the intense debates in the early church about the criteria for salvation: "Running through the NT are echoes of debates in the early church regarding the requirements for salvation and who will be saved." Noting a visible clash between Paul/Paul's followers and James over faith/confession vs. works for salvation, Culpepper comments, "[Matt] 7:21 rejects the sufficiency of the confession, 'Lord, Lord,' true and right though it may be."

Overall, Jesus exhorts his followers to obey God's will out of a humble, meek, just, merciful, pure heart that is seeking God's kingdom. This would define a "Christian" not simply as someone who believes certain doctrines but as somebody who lives a certain kind of life. This is not how Christianity is defined in many churches.

The SM ends with one last famous metaphor—building your house on a rock rather than on sand. At one level, this simply reinforces the overall teaching that our deeds matter to God. When the "house" (that is, our life) is examined, God will determine whether it was built on rock or sand, and only the house built on rock will "stand" on the judgment day.

But it can also be treated as a prudential statement, a kind of wisdom saying. Jesus teaches the Way, a way of life. Many other ways of life have been proposed, have been adopted. Many, many people attempt to build their lives on what amounts to sand. Those lives often collapse. Lies, violence, greed, pride, worry, lust, vengeance—these are not a great formula for a flourishing life. Davies and Allison put it starkly: "The house, symbolizing a person, has collapsed in condemnation, and the ruin is total."[3]

Jesus' teaching is not just eschatological or about salvation. It is an expression of love. Jesus gives us these teachings because he knows what kind of life works, what manner of living leads to joy, peace, justice, and covenant love. And after all, as we are told in John 1 and Col 1, Jesus Christ was the one through whom and for whom creation was made, the one in whom creation holds together. Since the one doing the teaching is the one who created, all in love, these teachings represent the wisdom of the Creator for human life. Good news indeed.

3. Davies/Allison Jr., *Matthew*, 724.

22

Whom to Fear

Do not fear those who kill the body but cannot kill the soul; rather, fear the one who can destroy both soul and body in hell.

—MATT 10:28

Texts: Matt 10:26–33/Luke 12:1–9

MATTHEW 10 IS AN entire chapter devoted to preparing the apostles for their first independent missionary journey. Jesus summons the Twelve and gives them authority (*exousia*) to conduct the kind of exorcism and healing ministry that he has been conducting (10:1). This particular word for authority means "power" or "dominion." It's the same word used by Jesus when he says he has authority over what is clean and unclean, and the same word that Matthew uses when he says Jesus taught with authority. (There are different Greek words that mean something more like "to command" or "to rule" that get translated as authority in English NT translations as well.)

The Twelve are named for the reader (Matt 10:2–4). These men are given instructions: this is to be a ministry exclusively to "the lost sheep of the house of Israel" (Matt 10:6). Their proclamation is to be of the kingdom of heaven. They are to accept no payment, but instead are to respond to hospitality or its lack (Matt 10:5–15).

Negative responses, including intimate betrayals, public trials, vicious floggings, slander before Jews and gentiles, all kinds of persecutions, are to be anticipated (Matt 10:16–25). They will be hated, rejected, even accused of being demonic, but so, says Jesus, is he. After all: "The disciple is not above the teacher, nor a slave above the master" (Matt 10:24)—e.g., the Twelve will share his reputation and his fate. Their calling is to "endure to the end" (Matt 10:22). Only those who do so will be saved. Jesus is readying his disciples not just for this current ministry but for future persecution unto death.

This prepares us for our focus passage here. The moral question seems to be a psychological, interpersonal, and spiritual question. It is a matter of fear. The question is not whether the disciples will be afraid. The question is whom they should fear.

Three times Jesus says, "be not afraid" (cf. Jer 10:5). He urges that his followers should not fear those who would inflict grievous harm. All these enemies can do is kill the body. They cannot touch the "soul" (*psychē*)—a word which can just as easily be translated "self." (This is where we get our word *psyche*.)[1] They cannot touch the core inner self if we don't let them. If we don't surrender that self to them, they can't get to it.

That core inner self belongs to God, and it is therefore only God whom we should fear. Surely that is the proper interpretation of Matt 10:28, unless we think that Satan has control over eternal judgment. God is the one from whom all humans come and to whom all humans will give an account. Fear only God—not people.

Many people have indeed been taught to fear God—more in past generations than today, but it is part of our religious heritage. Some have been taught a traumatizing fear of a God who dangles sinners over a pit of fire while angrily contemplating eternal judgments of human life.

Jesus wants us to fear disobeying God rather than displeasing people. But he surrounds the teaching with words of encouragement about the character of God. This is the God who sees all things and unveils all secrets (Matt 10:26). That is a soothing word to a persecuted church—the truth about their innocence will be revealed, as will the grotesque wrongs being done. That, at least, is one interpretation of this saying, which must have floated independently in the oral tradition of the early church and could be used in different ways (cf. Luke 8:17 and Luke 12:2).

---

1. Culpepper, *Matthew*, 206: "*Psychē* denotes the seat and center of the inner human life in its many and varied aspects."

Dietrich Bonhoeffer explains Matt 10:26 in this way: "Whatever happens to them now in secret will not remain in secret, but will be revealed before God and the people. The most secret suffering inflicted on them has the promise to be revealed as a judgment over the persecutors and as glory for the messengers."[2]

We are to fear only displeasing God. But this is the God who values even the sparrows, and values us so much more (cf. Matt 6:26), the God who numbers even the hairs of our head (Matt 10:29–31). This is the God who watches us for the boldness and courage of our proclamation in the teeth of intimidation, threat, and persecution (Matt 10:32–33). Matthew is imploring his disciples to proclaim their message freely despite threats intended to silence them. The main thing is to stand fast, and not deny Jesus when the powers of this world place all their intimidating force against us.

Bonhoeffer put it this way: "Human beings should not be feared. They cannot do much to the disciples of Jesus. Their power stops with the disciples' physical death. The disciples are to overcome fear of death with fear of God . . . Anyone who is still afraid of people is not afraid of God. Anyone who fears God is no longer afraid of people."[3]

Bonhoeffer wrote in Nazi Germany in the mid-1930s. Already many thousands had gone to Nazi prison cells and the early concentration camps. Among these were some resistant Christians. It was not yet the time of mass killing, but Nazi tyranny was strengthening, and Bonhoeffer knew that martyrdom was a very real possibility for anyone who stood firmly against Hitler. Bonhoeffer was already attempting to prepare church leaders who would resist Nazism to the death.

In any context of state tyranny over conscience, especially religious conscience, this "time of decision," as Bonhoeffer puts it, finally comes.[4] Those under the thumb of oppressive state power either decide to fear the state and surrender to its dictates, or to fear something higher and greater, such as a sovereign God or the demands of moral conscience.

Oppressive states want moral surrender more than they want martyrs (with genocide, of course, the ultimate exception). They want to break the spirit of the opposition. With the sufficient exercise of state terror, most ordinary human beings find their spirits indeed broken. Only a transcendent

2. Bonhoeffer, *Discipleship*, 196. The direct application to the torments being inflicted on Christian (and other) dissenters in Nazi Germany is painfully clear.

3. Bonhoeffer, *Discipleship*, 196.

4. Bonhoeffer, *Discipleship*, 197.

reference point, an ultimate accountability higher than the state, can equip people to become unbreakable in their spirits. Only if God becomes the one Reality does state terror become less real and therefore more bearable. This is the testimony of the martyrs of all ages.

Howard Thurman makes essentially the same point in his *Jesus and the Disinherited*. Fear comes naturally under racist oppression, Thurman says, and so does hatred of those who hate and oppress us for no reason. It is only the knowledge of God's love for us, the infinite value that God places on our lives, the dignity that this confers, the strength, hope, and perseverance that follow, only this allows us not to be broken under the wheel of racist oppression.[5]

You cannot make us fear you in any ultimate sense because we know who we are in God's love. This is Thurman's rendering of Jesus' message, as directed to the fearfulness of the disinherited. You cannot make us lie to you out of our fear of you. No fear of you will be allowed to motivate what we do. The body you may kill, but you cannot take our souls, which belong to God alone.

Fear only God (who is so very trustworthy and kind). Never fear a human being. This is a profoundly significant moral teaching of Jesus, applicable from grade school fears of the playground bully to a citizen facing the most tyrannical state power. It is a moral teaching of God-centered defiance. Many of the martyrs of history were equipped by this teaching to remain faithful even unto death.

5. Thurman, *Jesus and the Disinherited*, chs. 2, 4.

23

Wheat and Weeds

Let both of them grow together until the harvest.
—MATT 13:30A

Text: Matt 13:24–30, 36–43

AT FIRST GLANCE, THIS is not a "moral teaching of Jesus." It is one in a series of parables about the kingdom of heaven (see ch. 1 above), assembled in Matt 13: the parable of the sower (Matt 13:3–9, 18–23), then our parable of the wheat and weeds, the parable of the mustard seed (Matt 13:31–32), the parable of the yeast (Matt 13:33), the parable of the pearl of great value (Matt 13:45–46), the parable of the great catch of fish (13:47–50), and finally the parable comparing the scribes of the kingdom to a householder bringing out of his treasure new and old (13:51–52).

So why pick this parable of the wheat and tares (or weeds, in newer translations) for special consideration? It's because of the historical and still important use of this specific parable to teach a certain vision for how Christians should think about history, evil, and plurality of convictions.

This is a rare parable indeed in the way Jesus gives a complete object-by-object explanation rather than leaving a single thing to interpretation. The Son of Man (Jesus) is the one who sows good seed in the field, which is identified as "the world." In this parable, the good seed is not a message, but "the children of the kingdom" (13:38). The "weeds" are sowed by "an enemy"—the devil—these weeds are "the children of the evil one."[1]

So, Jesus and the devil are both sowers in the field that is the world. The result is a mix of good and bad people, symbolized in the parable as wheat and weeds. They "grow up" all mixed together in the world. This makes the field that is the world an unsightly and messy place. The servants ask the householder whether they should attempt to pull out the weeds that are messing up the garden. The householder tells them they should not, because in so doing they would risk pulling up the wheat as well. "Let both of them grow together until the harvest" (Matt 13:30).

But there indeed will be a harvest, which Jesus identifies as "the end of the age" (13:40). At that harvest, when the wheat is fully ready, and the weeds are right there with them, the reapers (identified by Jesus as angels), will finally do the separating that has been delayed to this point. "All causes of sin and all evildoers" will be harvested and then burnt in the "furnace of fire, where there will be weeping and gnashing of teeth" (13:41–42). Then the righteous children of the kingdom "will shine like the sun in the kingdom of their Father" (13:43). It is interesting that death is sometimes personified as the Grim Reaper. This reaping is pretty grim, especially for the weeds/bad people.

This parable can be understood to offer a moral teaching in the following way. The world is a place where children of God and children of the evil one both dwell. Indeed, they dwell so closely with each other that to attempt to uproot the bad is to risk uprooting the good. Jesus also seems to suggest that in this age it is not always possible for human beings to determine who or what is "wheat" and who or what is "weed" (Matt 13:29).[2]

So: *we are directed to wait for harvest time,* the end of the age, when God's angels will do the assessment, sorting, reaping, and (where necessary) burning. This means no human beings are permitted to advance that timetable and take on that role. *We* do not do the reaping; we wait for God's angels to do it at the very end of time. Meanwhile, we grow accustomed to living alongside and among people whom we believe may be children of the

---

1. Culpepper, *Matthew*, 256, notes the stark dualism of this parable, reminiscent of "the Qumran scrolls and the Johannine writings." God vs. Satan, good vs. evil, children of the kingdom vs. children of the evil one, etc. This itself is morally problematic, but the problem may be addressed in the parable itself.

2. Culpepper, *Matthew*, 257: "The weeds (*zizania*) are probably darnel, which is so similar to wheat that it can be readily distinguished only when they are ripe."

evil one. Perhaps we also accept the possibility that at the end of time there may be some very real surprises as to who is considered wheat and who is considered weeds (cf. Matt 25:31–46). In any case, it is not our call to make. We live in the world, as best we can, as "children of the kingdom" (Matt 13:38), and we wait for God to do the judging at the end.

This teaching has the implication that there will indeed be a harvest day in which evil is identified and evildoers are judged. This is comforting to the extent that our sense of justice is routinely frustrated by the evil, and evildoers, that run rampant in this world—a world that, after all, belongs to a good God who has a right to rule and who surely does not look kindly on all the mayhem, viciousness, and harm that happens here. The promise of the eschaton is that God's world will be restored to God's rule; this requires a reaping and a judging, that at last the world will arrive at the joyful wholeness for which we long.

So that day is coming—but not yet. We are taught an ethics of waiting for the one true God to be the one true Judge. This teaches humility and patience, core discipleship virtues. We are also taught a kind of tolerance, one that has proved crucial for Christians as we have gradually learned to accept the religious and moral diversity of the world. This is not a relativist tolerance, in which there is no "good" and "evil," but a Christ-centered, kingdom-of-God-type tolerance, in which there is indeed real good and real evil now, awful rebellion to be overcome and lovely wholeness to be achieved, but this through an ultimate reckoning by God alone.

The early Baptists of the seventeenth century were among the first modern Christians to see the crucial potential of this text to support religious toleration in both the church and the state. After many centuries of Christians persecuting other Christians, and Christian states using their coercive and violent powers to kill heretics, schismatics, and unbelievers, and in a Reformation-era context of brutal religious wars, the baptistic reading of this text was crucial.

The wheat and the weeds, the good and the bad, will be sorted. Check. *But not by us, and not now.* So: stop the killing! And more: create countries in which religious and moral differences are not punishable by law, and write constitutions in which religious liberty is protected. Not because there is no right or wrong, or truth or error, but because it is not our task to do the ultimate judgment thereof! This was a breakthrough, and a whole lot less killing in God's name took place on this earth once it was made.

One last point: in this parable, Jesus does still appear to have his listeners divide the world into children of the kingdom and children of the devil (however, again, cf. Matt 13:29). He does propose a binary of "righteous" ones and evildoers. Many of us are reluctant these days to talk that way about other people. Consider the insight in Aleksandr Solzhenitsyn's statement from *The Gulag Archipelago*: "The line separating good and evil passes not through states, nor between classes, nor between political parties either—but right through every human heart."[3]

This observation retains the reality of good and evil but refuses to identify the one or the other entirely with any group of people. That line runs "right through every human heart," so—much like Jesus' teaching in Matt 7 about judging—our moral work on earth is not about judging who is good and who is evil, but attending to the battle between the two that goes on within ourselves (cf. Matt 7:1–5). Could it be that each of us—including those of us who are committed Christians—are a field in which the devil and God, or evil and good, are daily doing battle?

3. Solzhenitsyn, *Gulag Archipelago 1918–1956*, 615–16.

24

Workers in the Vineyard

But he replied to one of them, "Friend, I am doing you no wrong; did you not agree with me for a denarius? Take what belongs to you and go; I choose to give to this last the same as I give to you. Am I not allowed to do what I choose with what belongs to me? Or are you envious because I am generous? So the last will be first, and the first will be last."

—*MATT 20:13–16*

Text: Matt 20:1–16

THE TRADITION OF INTERPRETATION in which most Christians have been immersed reads this parable entirely at a spiritual or soteriological (salvation) level, with a dollop of theological anti-Judaism thrown in. It is a parable of the "kingdom of heaven" (Matt 20:1), and thus it has been argued that it is a parable about who is accepted by God to enter eternal life.

On this reading, the landowner is God, and the vineyard is God's people Israel—the latter based on plenty of Hebrew Bible precedent (Isa 5; Jer 12:1–4). The long-serving workers in the vineyard are the Jewish people, or perhaps Jewish leaders like scribes, Pharisees, and priests. The late arrivers are believers in Jesus Christ. They are being welcomed into the vineyard by God's grace (not by Torah-keeping) and are being paid the same wage (salvation) as those who have been there all along. This strikes the long-timers as unfair. But from God's perspective, there is nothing unfair about God graciously deciding to pay the same "wages" to the late arrivers.[1]

I want us to set aside that interpretation and try something that is not anti-Jewish and does not overlook the economic ethics of this parable.

In our parable of the workers in the vineyard, it is not a matter of rejection of the original workers or violence against anyone. It is about late-comers being added to the labor force and paid the same as those who have been there far longer.

From the perspective of those who have labored all day, most of the day, or half of the day, the central issue is the fairness of being paid the same wage as those who only labored for one hour (Matt 20:11-12). But from the perspective of the owner, at least as this text sums it up, the issue is his freedom to do what he chooses with what belongs to him. He has paid the original workers the agreed wage, and he has paid all later-arriving workers the same wage. This is his prerogative as the employer (Matt 20:13-14). The all-day workers are at fault for being envious—interestingly, the literal Greek for Matt 20:15b is "Is your eye evil?" which takes us back to the teaching about covetous "bad eyes" in relation to money in Matt 6:22-23.[2]

Miguel De La Torre adds a crucial perspective to the reading of this parable.[3] It hinges on the denarius—the daily wage—and the life situation of day laborers in so many cultures. It took a denarius to support oneself and one's family for one day.[4] Day laborers had no guarantee of employment on any given day. If they did not work, they and their families more than likely did not eat. We see this still in much of the world: many day laborers wait outside in strategic locations beginning early in the morning in the hope that they will be hired for work that day. If they are not hired, or hired for only part of the day, or not paid enough, or not paid at all, they and their families will endure another day of hunger.

1. Culpepper, *Matthew*, 375–76, concurs: "Care must be taken . . . not to read this parable as a Christian condemnation of Judaism for legalism, contrasting grace and merit."

2. Brown, "Gospel of Matthew," in Blount, *True to Our Native Land*, 110.

3. De La Torre, *Politics of Jesús*, 102–9.

4. It is very difficult to calculate monetary equivalents between the Bible and our time. Culpepper, *Matthew*, 372, cites recent research suggesting greater earning power than this for the denarius, perhaps three to six days' worth of expenses for a family. However, this pay also had to cover taxes and debt.

From the perspective of a day laborer, *what matters is earning enough money on a given day to care for one's family* on that day. In the economic system Jesus describes in the parable, the expectation appears to be that only those who work twelve hours in "the scorching heat" (Matt 20:12) will earn enough to support their families for that day. Those who work fewer hours, or zero hours—not because they don't want to work more, but because no one has hired them (Matt 20:7)—still need the denarius to feed their families. The need doesn't change just because they have not been hired. Not receiving that denarius, they and their children will go hungry. As De La Torre writes: "Whether or not they were chosen to work that day, they still needed a full day's wage to meet their basic needs: food, shelter, clothing."[5]

Remember Jesus teaching his disciples to pray for daily bread. This parable reveals the social location and economic context in which such a prayer makes perfect sense.

The generosity of the employer in this parable may be seen as Jesus showing a very sympathetic understanding of the reality of day-laborer life. However long these men work each day, they need a denarius to feed their families that day. Rather than hewing to the logic of a meager hourly wage, leading to not enough pay for anyone who is not hired by 6 AM, the landowner instead *chooses an economic logic based on the need of the workers.* As De La Torre puts it, he feels a sense of responsibility to provide for his workers a "living wage," not a strict hourly wage that will leave some short of being able to feed their families.[6] This is generous—too generous, from the perspective of weary, jealous, sweaty, all-day workers—but it is based on a true assessment of the workers' needs and a counter-profit-motive understanding of the responsibilities of employers to workers.

We grow accustomed to daily needs going unmet in most societies. We accept the cruel logic of the marketplace, with its many unemployed people—and its many employed ones who are not paid enough to support themselves or their families, even if they work full-time. We are tolerant of societies in which a few people make millions (or billions) while many more must choose between food, heat, and health care.

In Jesus' perspective, the economic system exists to serve people; people don't exist to serve whatever economic system has been created. In this teaching about workers in the vineyard one can hear the echo of Jesus' teaching about the Sabbath (Mark 2:23—3:6, see ch. 2 above), and indeed,

5. De La Torre, *Politics of Jesús*, 104.

6. De La Torre, *Politics of Jesús*, 107.

his overall message about the relation between law, tradition, and justice (see ch. 4 above). The legal, economic, religious, and moral systems of this earth must serve human well-being, or they should be reconsidered and, if necessary, replaced.

The Catholic Church's social teaching tradition claims that God has provided abundantly on this earth for the needs of all and intends the "universal destination" (universal distribution) of enough goods for all. If all are not getting enough, then the problem is with our system, not with God or with the poor. All this feverish economic activity that consumes so much of our attention can distract us from the most basic thing—people need to eat, drink, and have housing. We need to set up an economy where everyone has enough.

That appears to be what the employer in this story understands. Whether Jesus also intended to tell a story about who will be included in eternal life is up for debate. Perhaps he was doing that too. But the story he chose to tell shows great insight into the injustices of economic life and about one landowner who saw things upside-down and thus right-side-up. I agree with Miguel De La Torre that Jesus certainly intended to teach something about what economic life looks like from the perspective of the kingdom of God—a kingdom of justice, love, and mercy. In the kingdom of God, finally, no human system is allowed to exist that deprives people of what they need to live.

PART THREE

Luke

25

The Anointing of Jesus

Therefore, I tell you, her many sins have been forgiven; hence she has shown great love. But the one to whom little is forgiven loves little. Then he said to her, "Your sins are forgiven." But those who were at the table with him began to say among themselves, "Who is this who even forgives sins?" But he said to the woman, "Your faith has saved you; go in peace."

—LUKE 7:47–50

Texts: Luke 7:36–50/Matt 26:6–13/Mark 14:3–9/John 12:1–8

THE STORY OF A woman who anoints Jesus with expensive ointment is one of the rare examples of an event that makes it into all four Gospels. Clearly, it was a memorable occasion and was viewed as significant. But it also offers a good example of a story whose details are edited in different ways by the four Gospel writers.

One key difference is where this story is placed in Jesus' life. Mark, Matthew, and John all place it during passion week. For Matthew and Mark, it is two days before Passover—and Jesus' arrest and crucifixion. For John, it is six days before. Only Luke places this story earlier in Jesus' ministry.

Mark, Matthew, and John all locate this event in Bethany, a stone's throw from Jerusalem. Mark and Matthew name the host as (the otherwise unknown) Simon the leper. John makes the host Mary, Martha, and Lazarus—Jesus' very close friends.

In Mark and Matthew, the one who anoints Jesus with "very costly ointment" is unidentified. In John, it is the hostess Mary herself, who has already demonstrated a spiritual and contemplative nature and close ties with Jesus. In Luke, it is "a woman in the city, who was a sinner" (Luke 7:37). We will return to this crucial point later.

The cost of this ointment is identified in Mark and in John as three hundred denarii, a vast amount. In Matthew, Mark, and John, it is the vast expense and waste of a major resource that could have been given to the poor that is seen as problematic and evokes the anger, scolding, and complaint. Only in John is the issue raised by the disciple Judas, who is identified infamously (only here), as the keeper (and embezzler) of their common purse (John 12:6). Notice that in Matthew and Mark, Judas goes immediately afterwards to betray Jesus, as if he has been outraged beyond the breaking point.

It should be noted that in both Mark and Matthew's account, the woman anoints Jesus' head, like how prophets anointed kings. This could be seen as a prophetic act recognizing the kingship of Jesus. In John and in Luke, Mary/the woman anoints Jesus' feet and then wipes them with her hair. The *Women's Bible Commentary* points out that feet were not usually anointed except for burial.[1]

In Matt, Mark, and John, Jesus responds to the complaint about the waste by declaring some variation of this line: you will always have the poor with you, but you will not always have me. He also explicitly describes what is happening as him being anointed in advance for his burial. Rather than being criticized for waste, the woman who has done this should be honored. That is in Matthew and Mark.

Putting together the accounts in Mark, Matthew, and John, the woman honors Jesus on the eve of his cruel execution by symbolically anointing his head for kingship and his body for burial, in advance. For these three Gospels, the reason the woman has anointed Jesus is because she prophetically understands who Jesus really is and that he is about to die a cruel death.

1. Jane D. Schaberg and Sharon H. Ringe, "Gospel of Luke," in *Women's Bible Commentary*, 505.

Her act is an expression of understanding where events were moving, expressing faith in and love for Jesus, and doing a kindness for his physical body—the last kindness it will receive. In John, the woman is Jesus' friend Mary. Perhaps one could more readily understand such an intimate act from a close friend. In Matthew and Mark she is unnamed. Yet she understands who Jesus is, what is going on, and what is fitting to do at that moment far better than the scolding disciples do. Normally, yes, you don't spend a year's wages this way. But the Messiah does not get crucified every day.

The moral teaching of this first iteration of the anointing story is that the right thing to do is sometimes only apparent in the situation. General moral rules—be a good steward of resources, give generously to the poor—are sometimes overridden by the demands of a particular situation, in this case the honor and care deserving of the suffering Messiah. Even Jesus—such a friend to the poor—agreed that while the poor would be there next week and could be helped, he would not (Mark 14:7).

Luke, however, has so entirely repurposed the story (assuming it is a description of the same event) that it carries a completely different meaning. Everything other than the account of a woman rubbing expensive ointment over Jesus has been changed. In Luke's account, the event is early in Jesus' ministry, in Galilee. The dinner is held at the home of a Pharisee, who has invited Jesus to dine with him. It is a public event.

The woman who enters uninvited is identified sparingly but devastatingly as "a sinner" (Luke 7:37).[2] It was tradition rather than the NT that identified her as Mary Magdalene. Her sin is not named. Christian tradition has tended to interpret her sinful reputation as something sex-related. Jane Schaberg and Sharon Ringe argue that "It is likely that Luke means the audience to identify this woman's sin as notorious sexual activity, prostitution."[3] But this is an inference only, and the matter remains disputed among biblical scholars.

The woman's ministrations to Jesus are described in detail. He is reclining at the table, and she stands behind him where he cannot see her. She weeps so copiously that she is described as bathing his feet with her tears. She uses her hair to dry his feet—the feet that she has wept on. So many tears. She kisses his feet, then she puts the ointment on them (Luke

---

2. Green, *Gospel of Luke*, 308–9, remarks, "[T]he woman's presence has introduced a powerful contagion, ritual impurity, into these goings-on . . . Everything about this woman . . . is wrong; she does not belong here."

3. Schaberg/Ringe, "Gospel of Luke," in *Women's Bible Commentary*, 505.

7:38–39). The woman is making quite a scene, and Jesus is saying nothing about what is going on.

Simon the host (a Pharisee, not the person with leprosy of the other accounts) responds with religious contempt. "He said to himself, 'If this man were a prophet, he would have known who and what kind of woman this is who is touching him—that she is a sinner'" (Luke 7:39). The word the Pharisee uses for "touch" is *haptomai*, which can mean "fasten to," "take hold of," or "to know carnally." There are two other Greek words for touch: *thiggano* (to manipulate, with a connotation of violence or violent intent), and *psallo* (to play an instrument, notice the similarity to the word *psalm*) that the Pharisee could have used to describe the woman's action; neither of them appear to carry any sexual connotation.

It certainly seems as if the Pharisee is interpreting the scene in front of him in a sexualized manner. NT scholar Joel Green writes, "Within her cultural context . . . all the more given her apparent reputation as a prostitute—her actions on the whole would have been regarded (at least by men) as erotic."[4] The Pharisee sees a fallen woman engaged in an intimate act and thinks Jesus must have little spiritual discernment if he can't see the same thing. He certainly cannot be a prophet.[5]

But Jesus interprets her actions very differently. By telling a brief parable of great gratitude for debts forgiven (Luke 7:41–42), Jesus interprets her actions as both hospitality that exceeds his host's very minimal hospitality,[6] and as enacted repentance—to which Jesus responds with a public pronouncement of forgiveness for "her sins, which were many" (Luke 7:47). He concludes the exchange with "Your faith has saved you; go in peace" (Luke 7:50).

A woman of ruined reputation in a small Jewish town has seen something in Jesus' ministry that has led her to believe that he is a bearer of divine grace.[7] She crashes a party at a Pharisee's house to encounter Jesus personally. She has an item of great value—that fine "alabaster jar of ointment" (Luke 7:37), which she has brought with her. She has a plan to offer it to the needs of Jesus.

---

4. Green, *Gospel of Luke*, 310.

5. Gadenz, *Gospel of Luke*, 150.

6. Gadenz, *Gospel of Luke*, 150.

7. Green, *Gospel of Luke*, 313, suggests an earlier encounter between Jesus and the woman, "the effect of which was her forgiveness."

The woman somehow knows who he is. She has faith in him. While the Pharisees are still checking him out by asking him questions over dinner, she is expressing her faith in him in the most public way. In her grief over her life, she weeps. In her gratitude for who Jesus has shown himself to be, she kisses his feet. In her desire to bless Jesus who embodies mercy and the presence of God, she anoints him. She shows love to him in the best way she knows how.

Jesus gets it. He does not accept any other interpretation of her actions than that she is repenting and believing and honoring him, and through this act reaching out to God. By virtue of her repentance, her sins are forgiven, and he says so in front of everyone (Luke 7:48–50).

I picture all these men around the table simultaneously objectifying and condemning this woman who has broken into their dinner party. Jesus, however, experiences a broken human being in the act of repentance, and he offers forgiveness. He experiences her great love, and he returns great love.

Now there's a moral teaching. Don't objectify or reject another person, especially in the name of God. Instead, offer pure, kind, merciful love to the human being in front of you.

26

The Greatest Commandment

You shall love the Lord your God with all your heart and with all your soul and with all your strength and with all your mind; and your neighbor as yourself.

—LUKE 10:27

Texts: Luke 10:25–37/Mark 12:28–34/Matt 22:34–40

HERE WE REACH WHAT can readily be described as the moral center of Jesus' teachings, or at least as a very serious candidate for that designation. Matt 22:34–40, Mark 12:28–34, and Luke 10:25–37 are parallel passages describing the same incident. In each version, a Jewish religious expert stands up and publicly addresses a question to Jesus. In Mark/Matt the question is essentially identical, focusing on which is the greatest command of Torah. In Luke, perhaps adapting for the gentile audience, the question is "What must I do to inherit eternal life?"

The answer in each case is the same. In Matt/Mark, Jesus gives the answer. In Luke, Jesus responds to his question with a question, so in the end the lawyer states the ancient precepts. In all cases, the answer is found by pulling together Deut 6:5 and Lev 19:18, pairing them as the greatest commandments, the path to eternal life. Love God with all you have and love your neighbor as yourself.

Endless commentaries have been written about this crystalline statement of what God requires of human beings. I would suggest we notice the following:

- The obligation is stated positively, in terms of what we *must* do, not negatively, in terms of what we must *not* do. This marks a break with the Decalogue but has its precedent in the Hebrew Bible, where Jesus finds these statements.

- As noted briefly in chapter 20 above, positive obligations are harder to meet than negative prohibitions. They open upward, always and indefinitely. Only a very foolish and prideful believer would ever say that they have fully achieved these obligations.

- This being the case, Jesus could be described as offering a counsel of moral perfection and therefore of impossibility, taking us back to the aspirational, high-ideals interpretation of his teachings. But before we head too far down that road, we need to see what Jesus does next in this passage. He does not speak as if he is teaching an impossibility.

- It is important that Jesus pairs love of God and neighbor. This invites interesting interpretive possibilities, like the following: we cannot love God if we do not love our neighbor. Or: the way we know we love God is through how we treat our neighbor. That's what the epistle 1 John repeatedly does with this teaching (cf. 1 John 2:10–11, 4:7–12). Or: we cannot love neighbor without the in-filling love of God that makes neighbor-love possible.

- Whatever move we make here, the linkage of love of God and neighbor stands as a permanent judgment against any version of Christianity in which love of God is claimed while harm of neighbor is practiced.

- Jesus, echoing Leviticus, tells us to love our neighbors *as ourselves*. This may mean—probably does mean—that Jesus is teaching that self-love is legitimate. But it may also mean that Jesus is taking for granted the inordinate love of self that so often characterizes fallen humanity, and simply saying—"You know how you love yourself and look after yourself so naturally? Direct that same kind of love to your neighbor!" The proper place of self-love has been an issue of confusion and much debate in a moral tradition whose founder taught and practiced sacrificial self-denial.

Only in Luke is the crucial additional question posed: "And who is my neighbor?" It is one of the most fateful questions in Scripture, and it never goes away in human life and in Christian ethics.

For the biblical context that might be driving the lawyer's question in Luke, it helps to consider Lev 19:17–18:

> You shall not hate in your heart anyone of your kin; you shall reprove your neighbor, or you will incur guilt yourself. You shall not take vengeance or bear a grudge against any of your people, but you shall love your neighbor as yourself: I am the Lord.

Most biblical scholars agree that in its original context this was a teaching about how fellow Israelites were to treat each other. The language of *your* kin, *your* neighbor, *your* people, resounds. This is an in-group moral obligation. It offers no obvious guidance for how to treat strangers. But just a few verses later (Lev 19:34), Israelites are told to "love the alien as yourself." As NT scholar Pablo Gadenz concludes, in asking who his neighbor was, the lawyer was responding to an OT legacy that "indeed suggested a range of options."[1]

Perhaps the lawyer just saw in Jesus a person whose vision was bigger than in-group loyalty. Or perhaps the lawyer himself yearned for a bigger vision. Or perhaps the lawyer really did want to know, in legal terms, precisely who counted in the category of neighbor. Because if God will judge us based on loving our neighbor as ourselves, it is imperative to know who counts as a neighbor.

And so, Jesus tells his now familiar story about the traveler in desperate trouble. Assaulted, robbed, stripped, left half-dead on the desolate and dangerous eighteen-mile road down from Jerusalem to Jericho, this unnamed man is utterly bereft and helpless. He will die if he is not given help. The priest and Levite see him but pass by on the other side, for reasons not specified but about which there has been much speculation.[2] From the perspective of the people left bleeding and helpless on life's roadsides, it does not really matter what the internal motivations are of those who pass

---

1. Gadenz, *Gospel of Luke*, 210.

2. Gadenz, *Gospel of Luke*, 211, Green, *Gospel of Luke*, 430, list the various theories, but Green rightly notes that "it is remarkable and probably significant that [Jesus offers] no inside information regarding the incentive(s) of the priest and Levite."

by on the other side. The only thing that matters is whether someone will come by who will stop and help.

That, of course, is what the Samaritan does. He sees—with compassion. He stops—and provides immediate first aid. Not just serving as the EMT, he also serves as the ambulance driver, carrying the helpless man to an inn. Not only that, but he also serves as an overnight nurse. Then he is the insurance company, providing payment for immediate and long-term care.

Jesus picks a Samaritan for his hero for an obvious reason if one knows the context. Samaritans and Jews were estranged half-brothers at a religious, ethnic, and national level. They were very uncomfortable near-neighbors—that is, neighbors by geography, not by sense of connection or moral obligation. Blood had been spilled between them.[3]

Glen Stassen and I argue in our book *Kingdom Ethics* that this story is our best example of Jesus defining love—and after all, that is what Jesus is doing here.[4] The lawyer wanted him to define neighbor, but instead Jesus defines love:

1. Love sees with compassion and enters into the situation of people in bondage.

2. Love does deeds of deliverance.

3. Love invites into community.

4. Love confronts those who exclude.[5]

To take this story as our paradigm, we could say that Jesus defines love of neighbor as *seeing with compassion* the suffering of wounded people—anyone who is hurting whose path we cross—then, *practicing merciful action* in concrete and needed ways, by purposefully including those who have been left in need into the safety and hospitality of community, and challenging all those who create the harms that leave people wounded by the side of the road. The lawyer summarizes all this with the word mercy, and Jesus does not dissent. He simply says: "Go and do likewise" (Luke 10:37).

Love requires insightful vision, heartfelt compassion, and effective action. It is a matter of doing, not of sentiment.

3. This background is discussed in Gadenz, *Gospel of Luke*, 212.

4. Gushee/Stassen, *Kingdom Ethics*, ch. 6, cf. 115–20.

5. That confrontation is implicit here, but in telling a story contrasting two men who did not include the wounded traveler in their community with another one who did, this marks an implicit confrontation of those who exclude.

Jesus' kind of love defines our neighbor as anyone whose path we cross, especially anyone in need. To be a neighbor means being the kind of person who offers mercy and therefore makes even a stranger into a neighbor—one whose life matters to us.

Here we do reach a summit in Jesus' moral teaching. It doesn't get any better than this. It also helps a very great deal that the one who offered this teaching went on to practice it with his life, and with his death. A key ingredient in the endless power of Jesus' teachings is that whenever we probe them deeply, and then look back up at the one who offered them, we see perfect congruence.

27

The Rich Fool

And he said to them, "Take care! Be on your guard against all kinds of greed, for one's life does not consist in the abundance of possessions."
—LUKE 12:15

Text: Luke 12:13–21

IN ANCIENT ISRAEL, PROBLEMS with inheritance were baked into Jewish Law (cf. Num 27:1–11, 36:7–9; Deut 21:16–17). The main legacy of most deceased in Israel was land, not money. Under the law of primogeniture, upon the death of the father, leadership in the family and a double share of the inheritance went to the eldest son. Single shares went to other sons. Fathers could choose to demote the firstborn son and elevate a later son if they wanted, ensuring absolute hatred between the two rival sons. Meanwhile, no shares went to daughters, who were instead provided with a dowry upon marriage. Daughters could only inherit if there were no sons.[1]

As our text opens, Jesus is being asked to weigh in on an inheritance dispute: "Someone in the crowd said to him, 'Teacher, tell my brother to divide the family inheritance with me'" (Luke 12:13).

1. Amy-Jill Levine, notes to "The Gospel According to Luke," in JANT, 141.

Two things could be going on here. One possibility is that the father has already died, and the elder brother has decided not to divide the estate immediately but to wait awhile. The other possibility is that the division of the estate has occurred, but the questioner, presumably the younger son, is unhappy with how the division has been made or with the overall unfairness of the whole system.[2]

Jesus responds with impatience: "Friend, who set me to be a judge or arbitrator over you?" (Luke 12:14).

Jesus did many things in his ministry, but he didn't take on inheritance disputes.[3] He knew what his ministry was about and was not distracted by other people's agendas. Instead of ruling on the dispute, he used the question to advance an agenda of his own kingdom ministry. He turns to the crowd and says this: "Take care! Be on your guard against all kinds of greed, for one's life does not consist in the abundance of possessions" (Luke 12:15).

A more literal rendering is found in the NASB, in which the second part of the verse reads: "For not [even] when one has an abundance does his life consist of his possessions."

This is a characteristic statement from Jesus, but we must not miss its radical force. The aggrieved younger brother wants justice. He wants *his share*, whether that which is due him under Torah or that which he thinks basic fairness requires.

Probably most of us would respond similarly. If we were being cheated out of an inheritance, we would protest. We would not likely respond very kindly to the implication that our actions are motivated by greed. We would say we are motivated by justice.

But Jesus is not interested in what we or his questioner think justice requires in this case. He is more worried about the state of the soul of the younger brother. It's a heart condition, called greed.

The Greek word here, *pleonexia*, means basically what we still mean by greed: insatiable desire, excessive or rapacious desire, the unsatisfiable quest for more, usually in relation to material possessions. This specific word, invoking the tenth commandment, can also be translated as "to covet." It carries the connotation of malice and bad intent. That can be contrasted with the word *epithumia*, which can be rendered the same way, but tends to be more like "to long" or "to desire." Something is going on with this young man that goes beyond basic longing.

2. Green, *Gospel of Luke*, 488.

3. Gadenz, *Gospel of Luke*, 239, notes the striking parallel to Exod 2:14.

Jesus is teaching that life is not found in abundance of possessions. The Greek word here, *zōē*, means fullness of life, real and genuine life, blessed life. To the inheritance-seeking younger brother, Jesus offers the warning that even if he wins, even if he gets what he is looking for, it will not make his life worth living.

To illustrate this point, he tells his famous story that we call the "parable of the rich fool." It is worth recounting in full:

> The land of a rich man produced abundantly. And he thought to himself, "What should I do, for I have no place to store my crops?" Then he said, "I will do this: I will pull down my barns and build larger ones, and there I will store all my grain and my goods. And I will say to my soul, Soul, you have ample goods laid up for many years; relax, eat, drink, be merry." But God said to him, "You fool! This very night your life is being demanded of you. And the things you have prepared, whose will they be?" (Luke 12:16–20)

Most of the people Jesus was talking to were probably poor subsistence farmers or day laborers. Most of the wealth was in the hands of a very small slice of the population. To that hungry audience, yearning for daily bread, this must have been a pleasing story.

A rich man is about to get richer because of a bumper crop. The rich man does not ask anyone around him what he should do with this bumper crop. He certainly does not ask anyone who might like a bit of that grain what he should do with it.[4] He does not think of sharing as an option. He does not consider selling at a deep discount to those who might need it desperately. This grain is *his*, and he alone will contemplate how to benefit from it.[5]

He decides to build bigger barns. He puts his feet up. He prepares to live in even more ease, comfort, and luxury than he has already been enjoying.

But then God says to him, "this very night your life is demanded of you" (Luke 12:20). In the Greek you can't tell who exactly is making this demand of the man's life. One of the possible readings is that it is the abundance itself that kills him. Another is that his life should have been understood as on loan from God, a loan that has now been called.[6] In any

---

4. Green, *Gospel of Luke*, 490: "[G]iven the high level of interconnectedness characteristic of the village economy, it is worth asking why this farmer lays out a course of action in isolation from others whose well-being is affected by this decision." Green also notes that "self-talk" like that of the rich fool is "consistently portrayed negatively by Luke."

5. Gadenz, *Gospel of Luke*, 239.

6. Gadenz, *Gospel of Luke*, 240.

case, all his plans amount to nothing, and all his accumulated stuff is now worthless to him.

This question—"whose will they be?"—reminds us of the darker parts of Ecclesiastes (cf. Eccl 2:15–21).[7] All this work, what will it lead to? You die and others get your stuff, the stuff you've worked so hard to accumulate. Death is the ultimate reminder that one's life does not consist in the abundance of possessions. We can't take that car, boat, wardrobe, or house to our meeting with God.

Jesus concludes with what we now can see is a very characteristic statement: "So it is with those who store up treasures for themselves but are not rich toward God" (Luke 12:21).

Once again, we hear Jesus contrasting treasures on earth vs. treasures in heaven, material riches for self vs. spiritual riches in the sight of God. The rich man stored up treasures on earth and riches for himself. But what God wants is being rich toward God and storing up treasures in heaven.

This could be individualized to read something like this: have a great devotional life, read the Bible, pray a lot. But from other Gospel passages and the Jewish background it is quite clear that riches toward God and treasures in heaven are accrued by serving others—especially the poor—especially with money and possessions. This parable is not just a wisdom parable signaling the old but always valuable lesson that *you can't take it with you*. It is a judgment parable about greed and its callous twin, disregard for the poor.

Those who live for stuff have a hard time living for others. There is not room in the heart for both loves.

Or, to put it positively, those who truly love their neighbors as themselves will be unlikely to love their stuff unduly. There is no place in their heart for such a lesser love.

The warning of the passage is explicit: watch out for greed.

The invitation is implicit: love what matters most. Love people, not stuff.

7. Levine, in JANT, 142.

28

Humility and Exaltation

For all who exalt themselves will be humbled, and those who humble themselves will be exalted.

—*Luke 14:11*

Texts: Luke 14:7–24, cf. Luke 18:14, Matt 22:1–14

JESUS NOTICES DINNER GUESTS jockeying for position at a party hosted by "a leader of the Pharisees" (Luke 14:7). It seems that many want "the places of honor" at the party, presumably on the host's right and left side—one thinks of James and John and their ambition to occupy such places of honor in Jesus' coterie, which we have already discussed (Matt 20:20–28 and parallels).

On a superficial reading, Jesus could seem to be simply offering instructions in etiquette here. The reason to begin the party by going to "sit down at the lowest place" (Luke 14:10) is so that you do not face the humiliation of being ejected from a better seat to a worse one in front of everyone (Luke 14:9), and so that you have the opportunity to "be honored in the presence of all who sit at the table with you" (Luke 14:11) when the host invites you to move on up the seating chart. Both to avoid dishonor and to possibly gain honor, go sit at the lowest seat. Nothing can go wrong for you there, while much can go right. For a similar idea, compare Prov 25:6–7.

But Jesus seemed to care little about etiquette, except for the far deeper, deeply twisted values it so often reveals.[1] In this first story about dinner party behavior, he teaches a lesson about the dialectic between exaltation and humility. In contexts in which insecure strivers constantly aim to claw their way to the top—that would be most contexts, with the full approval of society—Jesus teaches us not to be insecure, self-exalting strivers at all.

Instead, be humble, and completely opt out. Those trying so hard to be somebody will be brought low, while those who humbly know who they are—one might say *Whose* they are—have rejected the self-exaltation game altogether. They are immune to being brought low because they are already low; that is, they are not hinging their identity and worth on the approval of other human beings.

This teaching bears a resemblance to the earlier one that we saw about being afraid not of people but only of God. In Luke, it was just two chapters back (Luke 12:1–9). Jesus is such a shrewd analyst of the human heart. He knows that most people most of the time orient their lives around the approval of other human beings, striving mightily to be approved and fearing greatly to be disapproved. Entire cultures of shame and honor, including Jesus' own culture, are built on this primal drive for honor/approval/exaltation and fear of dishonor/disapproval/shame.

The only way out appears to be through a conscious, radical decision to seek our worth through God and not people. To draw one's identity from God and not from anyone else. To strive for the kingdom of God rather than my kingdom—or a high place in some other powerful kingdom. Secure in being humble before God, focused purely on God's will, striving solely for God's kingdom, we can recognize that human status games mean nothing. We are happy to humble ourselves now, confident that God will exalt us later.[2]

Note, once again, that Jesus always practices what he preaches. Try to think of any time—a single occasion, even one—in which Jesus ever jockeyed for social position or seemed anxious to gain approval from any human being. The one who humbled himself was exalted (cf. Phil 2:5–11).

---

1. Green, *Gospel of Luke*, 550: "When Jesus subverts conventional mealtime practices related to seating arrangements and invitations, he is doing far more than offering sage counsel for his table companions. Rather, he is toppling the familiar world of the ancient Mediterranean, overturning its socially constructed reality and replacing it with what must have been regarded as a scandalous alternative."

2. Gadenz, *Gospel of Luke*, 265, notes the absolute centrality of this message in Luke (cf. Luke 1:46–55, 18:14), and more broadly in the NT (cf. Phil 2:5–11).

The second dinner party teaching that we consider here takes the message of humility even further. Jesus instructs his host, and any who would have the means to throw a big luncheon or dinner, not to invite their friends or family, "in case they may invite you in return, and you would be repaid" (Luke 14:12). Instead, "invite the poor, the crippled, the lame, and the blind" (Luke 14:13). Why? "You will be blessed, because they cannot repay you, for you will be repaid at the resurrection of the righteous" (Luke 14:14).

Once again, Jesus is skewering worldly practices of hospitality.[3] Still today social occasions are often about demonstrating wealth and social position, such as the ability to pull off a big dinner party with a high-status guest list, and incurring social debts, such as creating the conditions in which those invited will need to return the invitation back your way. This is often how high-status people engage in social life, in an endless whirl of expensive invitations, which likely demonstrate wealth more than genuine affection. I don't care about you, but I must invite you, because you invited me to your last boring but expensive party. All this does is play status games, waste money and time, and exclude everyone who doesn't have the money to play the game—such as the poor, crippled, lame, and blind, the groups that Jesus names here.

Jesus once again teaches that only one reward is available for actions in this life—either a heavenly reward or an earthly reward, and the heavenly reward is the only one that matters. Just as he taught that we could do acts of piety either to be honored by people or by God, but not by both (Matt 6:1–18), so here he teaches that we can offer hospitality either for God's sake or for human approval, but not both. If we are offering hospitality for God's sake, we will invite those who cannot reciprocate, who cannot benefit us in any way. It will be added as a credit to our account with God, to be rewarded at "the resurrection of the righteous" (Luke 14:14b). That's the treasure in heaven concept, once again.

Jesus teaches a scale of values that is upside down from standard human values. Be humble rather than self-exalting. Invite low-status people rather than the elite. Take the lowest place rather than jockeying for the best seat. Seek God's approval rather than human approval. His radicalism is breathtaking in relation to this mess of a world that we humans have

---

3. Green, *Gospel of Luke*, 553, argues that what Jesus teaches "would sound the death knell for the ethics of patronage and, more generally, for the regulation of social affiliations according to the demands of reciprocity. The behaviors Jesus demands would collapse the distance between rich and poor, insider and outsider."

made for ourselves. From Jesus' perspective, our normal social values are corrupted and vainglorious.

In the next parable, of the great banquet (Luke 14:15–24/Matt 22:1–14), Jesus takes one final step. He is now using a parable to describe God's invitation to humanity to the great kingdom banquet that awaits on the other side of this world's transformation. In this story, the "master" (Luke 14:21) invites "many" to his "great dinner," but is met with "excuses" from the great and the good. So the master invites the same group of generally unwanted ones—"the poor, the crippled, the blind, and the lame" (Luke 14:21)—and then dragoons the highways and byways to get a full crowd for his banquet.

Here the idea reflects a common theme in Jesus' teaching, that the great and the good, the first and the expected, will be surprised to find themselves shut out of God's kingdom and replaced by the humble, the last, the least, the worthless in the eyes of the world. The last end up first, and the first last; the humbled are exalted, and the exalted humbled. Compare the congruence of this teaching with his statements in Luke 6:20–26: woe to you who are rich, laughing, honored, and invited to all the best parties now, for one day everything will be turned upside down.

It is as if Jesus is looking at every social gathering that he witnesses as a rehearsal for that great messianic banquet in the upside-down kingdom of God. And he suggests that we had better start thinking and acting in this same upside-down way if we wish to be ready for that day.

29

Lost Sons, Broken Family

*Then the father said to him, "Son, you are always with me, and all
that is mine is yours. But we had to celebrate and rejoice, because this
brother of yours was dead and has come to life; he was lost and has
been found."*

—LUKE 15:31–32

Text: Luke 15:1–32

THE THREE PARABLES ABOUT lost things here in Luke 15 are clearly framed
by the editor of the Gospel as parables of God's extravagant grace, exhib-
ited by Jesus through his table fellowship with "sinners" (Luke 15:2). Most
Christians have indeed been taught to read the stories as accounts of God's
magnificent grace especially to the most wretched sinners. NT scholar
Amy-Jill Levine also documents how the stories have been read in an
anti-Jewish way, to contrast Christianity's generous understanding of God's
grace with Judaism's harsh "legalism"—a significant weapon in the arsenal
of Christian anti-Jewish reading of the New Testament. This interpretation
needs to be abandoned.[1]

1. Levine, *Short Stories of Jesus*, 30. Gadenz, *Gospel of Luke*, 275, notes that Augustine
viewed the elder brother in the prodigal son story to represent "Israel" (which does not

The stories can be summarized in parallel in the following way. First a man loses one of one hundred sheep (Luke 15:4). He leaves the ninety-nine behind to go find the one, and after achieving success, returns home and gathers his friends to celebrate (Luke 15:4–6). Then a woman loses one of her ten silver coins (Luke 15:8). She turns her household upside down to find the one lost coin, and after finding it gathers her friends and throws a party (Luke 15:8–9). Finally, a man loses one of his two sons (Luke 15:11–13). When the lost son returns home, the man gathers his household for a big celebration (Luke 15:22–24).

Jesus closes the first two stories by teaching about the great joy in heaven over "one sinner who repents" (Luke 15:7, 10). Interestingly, though the father is joyful upon his son's return in the third story (Luke 15:22–24), there is no similar tidy ending, because not everyone in that household is rejoicing. Children are more complicated than sheep and coins, it appears.

The story commonly known as "the prodigal son" begins with a man who had two sons. Levine points out that readers of the Hebrew Bible will be thoroughly familiar with stories of a man who had two sons (Cain and Abel, Ishmael and Isaac, Jacob and Esau, Manasseh and Ephraim, for example).[2] These stories depict conflict, rivalry, and surprise. Often it is the younger son who is favored, against the grain of a system of primogeniture in which older sons are supposed to inherit the patriarch's mantle.

In this case, we do not know if the younger son has been similarly favored all along. We do know that the younger son asks his father to divide and distribute the property. The father does so, even though he is under no requirement. It seems that the father divides his assets evenly (suggested by Luke 15:12), which is not what is prescribed by Deut 21:17, where the eldest son typically received a double portion.[3] Levine says that in first-century Jewish practice this inheritance decision was ultimately left to the father.[4]

What do we make of the decision of the father to go ahead and distribute a significant chunk of his assets, at the son's request? It was certainly not required of him, and may signal an overindulgence of the younger son,

---

believe in Jesus), the younger brother to represent the gentiles who now do believe in Jesus. It is unfortunate that Augustine's interpretation is reported uncritically in this 2018 commentary.

2. Levine, *Short Stories of Jesus*, 50–51.

3. Gadenz, *Gospel of Luke*, 276, does not see an even division of the property here.

4. Levine, *Short Stories of Jesus*, 53.

reminiscent of the Joseph story (Gen 37–50).[5] Those who know that Joseph story will also know the resentment that Joseph's brothers felt.

Green notes that since the father "divided his property between them" (Luke 15:12), this means that the younger son's request has caused the father to go ahead and distribute the whole of his estate in advance of his death.[6] From my perspective as a father of grown children who will one day inherit the estate of my wife and me, it seems as if the younger son's request has more-or-less caused the father's premature economic/legal death. Henceforth, he will be something of a guest in his own (former) home.

The younger son, now freshly armed with plenty of shekels, leaves the household a few days later. We are not told whether this plan was known in advance to anyone else in the family, or if so what kind of conversations there would have been about it. It reads as a unilateral decision, and its lack of wisdom becomes apparent quickly, as he squanders this considerable wealth through "dissolute living" (Luke 15:13). The younger son has taken all his inheritance, cashed it out, and lost it in very short order.

Soon this child of wealth is hungry and desperate. He must take a job as a hired man, deployed to feed pigs—a nice Jewish boy must now feed unclean pigs in gentile country. Not good. He is hungry, but "no one gave him anything" (Luke 15:16).[7] The young man is desperate. He has earned his plight, though famine in the land has also played a role.

Destitute and desperate, he now "comes to his senses" (Luke 15:17). "Dying of hunger," he decides to return home, rehearsing his return speech to his father. Please just take me in as a hired man, not even as your son any longer. Is this repentance, as Christians commonly assert? Or is it the last option of a not-sorry but starving young man?

He returns home. His father, who seems to be depicted as regularly scanning the horizon for any sight of him, sees him and is "filled with compassion" (Luke 15:20). Surely, he saw a gaunt, weary, unwell looking young man, no longer the strutting peacock who so confidently had left home.

The father goes running out to see his son, throws his arms around him and kisses him (Luke 15:20). The son begins his long-rehearsed speech but is unable to get it all the way out before the father offers his famous

5. Levine, *Short Stories of Jesus*, 53.

6. Green, *Gospel of Luke*, 580.

7. Green, *Gospel of Luke*, 581, points out the younger son is in gentile territory, in which "the practice of almsgiving was little observed." People don't care if this young man starves.

interruption, directed to the servants—bring him the best robe, put a ring on his finger and sandals on his feet, kill the fatted calf, prepare a big party—because "this son of mine was dead and is alive again; he was lost and is found!" (Luke 15:24). At first the father reads as a compassionate man who sees a hungry son and does what any good parent would do—he takes him in and begins to take care of him. But his welcome back is extravagant in the extreme. The father has graciously begun the process of restoring the wastrel child who has dishonored him to the status of a celebrated son.[8]

In the striking end of the story, the older son comes home from working in the field, hears the party going on, gets the report from the servant, and angrily refuses to go in and join the meal, a hugely important snub signaling a breach in kinship (Luke 15:28).[9] The father comes out to him and pleads with him—Levine translates this as "comforted/urged him" (from *parakaleo*).[10]

Picture the fury on the older brother's face, before he even says a word. The father wants to calm his son, to comfort him, but also to exhort him—please join me in welcoming your brother. Please see how "we had to celebrate and rejoice" (Luke 15:32), because it as if we have received your brother back from the dead. Whether the older brother will get past his negative feelings about his brother, his resentment of his father's indulgent approach, his sense of himself as being overworked and underappreciated (Luke 15:29–30)—this we do not know.

The story is left open-ended, as regards the elder brother. This means it is not clear whether this family will be able to function as a family ever again. But the final words that Jesus offers—in the father's name but reflecting Jesus' own amazing grace, are these: "But we had to celebrate and rejoice, because this brother of yours was dead and has come to life; he was lost and has been found" (Luke 15:32). Jesus is in the lost-and-found business. Jesus throws parties for those who find their way back to God.

How shall we read this story? Parables resist single interpretations. The standard Christian interpretation is that God loves sinners extravagantly and goes looking for us when we stray. And when we are reclaimed, heaven itself resounds with joy. Jesus' own words reflect that.

---

8. Green, *Gospel of Luke*, 582.

9. Green, *Gospel of Luke*, 584–85.

10. Levine, *Short Stories of Jesus*, 68.

But at a moral level, I am struck by the way in which this story has not one but two lost sons, and a great deal of family brokenness.[11] It is a story about tensions in families, conflicts, rivalries, and the challenges of asking and offering forgiveness and finding reconciliation. It is a story about a father desperate to hold his fractured clan together. And where is the mother of these boys? Dad could use some help here!

Many readers will be able to identify with this story because of deeply conflictual and unresolved structural problems in their own families, dynamics of perceived favoritism, or unforgiven wrongdoing, or unjust financial or power relations. Maybe some can identify with dynamics being so bad that when one family member leaves, presumably forever, there is relief, not sadness—and if that person comes back, there is not celebration, only more stress and drama.

Noting that the elder brother doesn't want any part of a conversation with his younger brother and won't go to his party (indeed, won't even describe him as his brother), we see that if there is to be reconciliation in this family it will be a long journey. Will there be forgiveness for specific wrongs in the past? Or will the family simply have to resolve to move on together as a family, because that is what families sometimes must do?

The fatted calf party is for one evening. Whether it will be an evening leading to forgiveness, reconciliation, and family wholeness depends on the subsequent decisions of each of the characters in this story. That is often how it goes in life. Sometimes the unhealthy dimensions of our most important relationships break open with surprising possibilities of new life. But we must seize the moment. Amy-Jill Levine concludes: "Take advantage of resurrection—it is unlikely to happen twice."[12]

---

11. An idea suggested to me by reading Levine, *Short Stories of Jesus*, ch. 1.

12. Levine, *Short Stories of Jesus*, 75.

30

God vs. Mammon

You cannot serve God and Mammon.
—*Luke 16:13, RSV*

Text: Luke 16:1–15

LUKE TAKES AN ODD and often ignored parable of Jesus, which we call "the parable of the shrewd manager," and appends several other sayings to it, in an effort to explain a difficult story.[1]

In the parable, we quickly meet a wealthy landowner. This rich man has hired someone to manage his business. This manager is the highest-ranking employee and one with considerable autonomy over the owner's business affairs.

But he has not been handling the owner's business very well. He has been "squandering" his master's wealth. The Greek word *diaskorpizo* originated as an agrarian term. While it gets translated in this passage (and in Luke 15:13) as "squandering," the word tends to mean the same thing as the verb "to sow," as in scattering seed.

---

1. A similar treatment of this text, with extensive overlapping material, is offered in Gushee, *Introducing Christian Ethics*, ch. 16.

Someone blows the whistle on this manager, and he is about to be dismissed, at one blow losing his job, housing, and status. The manager then quickly makes the rounds of his master's debtors and starts offering discounted deals on their large debts. The size of the debts helps confirm the owner's great wealth. What the manager does is to reduce the master's "accounts payable" without his permission. He does this to create obligations toward himself on the part of the master's debtors. They now owe the manager hospitality or other service if he needs it, and it sure looks like he is going to need it.[2]

The surprise of the story is that in the end the master praises the manager, now described for the first time in v. 8 as *adikias* (unrighteous/unjust—often translated "dishonest"). His praise is because the manager has acted *phronimos*—a term usually translated as "shrewdly," but just as easily translated as astutely, practically, or prudently.

If we cut off the passage here, it seems that what we have is Jesus looking around at the world and describing one aspect of how it works. At the top of the economic pyramid are the rich landowners. They are experts at accumulating wealth, cutting deals, and leveraging their power.

Starting there, we can perhaps see how a rich landowner *who is in the process of being cheated by his household manager* could at the same time think him rather clever. That's because these are the kind of shrewd moves that the rich owner has himself made in his rise to the top. The likely end of this story is that the owner brings the manager back home. He gives him a stern admonition to stop wasting his money. But he also pats him on the back for his cleverness.

Can't you just picture a whole lot of peasant listeners all nodding their heads as they recall their own encounters with the shady economic practices of the powerful people of their world?

Everything from Luke 16:8b–15 seems to be Luke's attempt to interpret this parable of Jesus. He appends four other sayings of Jesus to do so. These efforts reveal the difficulty of making sense of the story but also give glimpses of the radicalism of Jesus' economic ethics. Let's take them one at a time:

1) Luke 16:8b–9: "For the children of this age are more shrewd in dealing with their own generation than are the children of light. And I tell you, make friends for yourselves by means of dishonest wealth (Gk: *mamonas ho adikia*), so that when it is gone, they may welcome you into the eternal homes."

---

2. Green, *Gospel of Luke*, 592–93.

NT scholar Joel Green's commentary suggests that Jesus is drawing a distinction between two ages: "this age" and the "age to come"—the kingdom age.[3] The inhabitants of the age to come are called "the children of light," implicitly contrasted with the unnamed "children of darkness" of this age. Jesus is calling together a community of children of light who for now dwell in a world ruled by children of darkness. What makes the children of light distinct is that they are working alongside Jesus to give birth to a new age—the kingdom of God.

The economic ethics of the children of darkness are predictably *adikos* (unjust). Jesus is saying that in this age, dominated as it is by the children of darkness, wealth acquisition is filled with injustice. The term the NRSV translates as "dishonest wealth" would be more literally translated as "Mammon of injustice," and that translation has much more bite to it. We saw earlier that the word Mammon is imbricated with idolatry. The use of the word Mammon here gives evidence of Jesus' perspective on the whole economic system.

Nowhere in the story does Jesus describe the economic practices of the rich landowner. But he implies that the landowner sits at the top of a system filled with injustice, dishonesty, and the shrewdness of a corrupt age, all in the service of the endless, idolatrous quest for wealth that dominates so many lives.

Mammonism has also gotten wired into cultural practices, so that table fellowship, friendship, and hospitality are tied to people's wealth, status, and indebtedness within the corrupt economic system. People who have the most resources use them to accrue status, acquire "friends," compete with one another, and create various kinds of social indebtedness. Meanwhile the poor go begging.

Note the pivotal reference to friendship in verse 9: "Make friends for yourselves by means of dishonest wealth, so that when it is gone, they may welcome you into the eternal homes." This may mean that Jesus is counseling his followers to use whatever access they might have to money to initiate relationships in which they can show a very different kind of friendship and build up a very different kind of treasure.

2) Luke 16:10–12: "Whoever is faithful in a very little is faithful also in much; and whoever is dishonest in a very little is dishonest also in much. If then you have not been faithful with the dishonest wealth, who will entrust

3. Green, *Gospel of Luke*, 593.

to you the true riches? And if you have not been faithful with what belongs to another, who will give you what is your own?"

The first statement could be read independently as a wise observation about human character, the way that it reveals itself in matters small and large. Someone who will cheat you out of a dollar in a poker game reveals plenty about himself. Here, Jesus is turning this observation into a move something like this: money means little in the economy of the kingdom. There are far higher and truer riches. But disciples prove their readiness to receive the true riches by whether they learn to handle "unjust Mammon" justly, in keeping with kingdom values.

3) Luke 16:13: "No slave can serve two masters; for a slave will either hate the one and love the other, or be devoted to the one and despise the other. You cannot serve God and wealth."

This text, which is also found in the Sermon on the Mount (Matt 6:24), is one of Jesus' most memorable sayings about wealth. Green tells us that in the Greco-Roman world, enslaved people *could*, in fact, be under the control of more than one master.[4] The issue, then, is about "the diametrically opposed forms of service" demanded by God and Mammon: "Since each grounds its demands in such antithetical worldviews, one cannot serve them both."[5] One cannot serve two masters whose demands are utterly contradictory.

4) Luke 16:14–15: "The Pharisees, who were lovers of money, heard all this, and they ridiculed him. So he said to them, "You are those who justify yourselves in the sight of others; but God knows your hearts; for what is prized by human beings is an abomination in the sight of God."

The Pharisees are described by Luke (not Jesus) as "lovers of money," a suggestion that is not historically supported.[6] Green suggests that in both Greco-Roman and Hellenistic Jewish circles this term (*philargyroi*) had become a stock phrase to describe self-glorifying false teachers.[7] Perhaps Luke's Jesus simply intends to accuse some Pharisees of participating in the money-based status games of the time rather than challenging them, which they should do as leaders of God's people. Or perhaps this insertion

---

4. Green, *Gospel of Luke*, 597.

5. Green, *Gospel of Luke*, 597.

6. Levine, in JANT, 122, reporting Josephus's account of the Pharisees' simple standard of living, especially by contrast with the Sadducees.

7. Green, *Gospel of Luke*, 601.

reflects the documented later tension between the Jesus communities and other Jewish groups, an unfortunate stereotype rather than Jesus' own view.

That last line, though, sums up the section and packs quite a wallop. "What is prized by human beings is an abomination in the sight of God." Everyone desires Mammon, but for Jesus, Mammon is not only unworthy of being desired, it is an abomination. That intense word, *bdelygma*, connotes something profane, unclean, polluted, and connected with idolatry.

Here is Joel Green's overall summary of Jesus' message: "According to Luke, the rule of Wealth is manifest in theft and exploitation, hoarding, conspicuous consumption, and the more general disregard for outsiders and persons of low status and need."[8] Those at the top of the economic pyramid exploit others to get there, consume excessively, hoard wealth, disregard the poor, and play a reciprocity-based social game.

Jesus, on the other hand, joins the disinherited of the earth in looking at his world's economic system as intrinsically unjust, and even as an idol called Mammon. He looks closely at the system, and the people who prosper in it, and the culture they have created around it, and sees something that can simply be summarized as *adikos*—unjust, or unrighteous. He asks those who would be his followers to work out a different relationship with money, and to make it just money again. He calls them to topple Mammon from its throne.

Jesus' critique of the economic system of his time is not reformist. It is more radical than that. Jesus seems to suggest that in this age dominated by the children of darkness, there is no redeeming economic life. We might put it this way: even though this world's economic systems feed many people and organize much of culture, they are drenched in collective human sin—sin that is especially dangerous because people take it for granted and often act as if success within this corrupt system offers evidence of their own virtue.

Jesus sees our vast economic structures for what they are, and with prophetic radicalism warns us about the evils that are baked into them. His is a far more radical vision than most Christians who have prospered in this world are willing to consider.

---

8. Green, *Gospel of Luke*, 596–97.

31

Lazarus and the Indifferent Rich Man

But Abraham said, "Child, remember that during your lifetime you received your good things and Lazarus in like manner evil things, but now he is comforted here, and you are in agony."

—LUKE 16:25

Text: Luke 16:19–31

WITH A BRISK BUT powerful economy of words, Jesus depicts a rich man, living the high life. As NT scholar Amy-Jill Levine points out, the parable sends several signals of extreme extravagance in one verse (Luke 16:19).[1] His purple clothes and fine linen were the most expensive available. He ate every day like it was a feast day.[2] There is no mention of a wife, a family, or anyone else. It appears to be the rich man and his household full of dutiful servants, helping him live his extravagant life. How this man's lifestyle looks from the perspective of the poor is quite obvious before we hear anything else about his behavior.

When talking appreciatively about John the Baptist earlier in Luke (7:25), Jesus offered an offhand but pungent comment about the rich:

---

1. Levine, *Short Stories of Jesus*, 272–73.
2. Gadenz, *Gospel of Luke*, 287.

"What, then, did you go out to see? Someone dressed in soft robes? Look, those who put on fine clothing and live in luxury are in royal palaces" (Luke 7:25).[3] This was classic Jesus-type populist economics—we out here who must pray for daily bread and who are lucky to have two items of clothing to cover our shivering bodies have an opinion about those who live in extravagance and indifference to the rest of humanity.

That is certainly what is going on here. But there is more. The rich man has an unimportant-to-him neighbor named Lazarus. Lazarus is a sick, hungry, defenseless, probably homeless poor man who lies at the rich man's gate—not begging, just fantasizing about eating his leftovers (Luke 16:20–21). But, as with the parable of the prodigal son, nobody appears to give Lazarus a thing—certainly not the rich man.

It is striking that Jesus gives Lazarus a name while leaving the rich man unnamed.[4] That is the first of several "great reversals" in this text. Rich men get buildings named after them, while the poor remain anonymous. But not here. It should be noted that the name Lazarus derives from the name Eliezer, which means "God helps" in Hebrew.[5] The name feels ironic, because in this life no one is helping Lazarus at all.

The rest of the story is a split-screen scene of eternal judgment. Lazarus appears to die first—of course, because he was hungry, sick, and exposed.[6] The one who had not been helped in life is now "carried away by the angels to be with Abraham" (Luke 16:22). The rich man also dies. Once again, great wealth, purple clothes, fine linen, filled barns, and fine food cannot prevent anyone's appointment with death.

The rich man finds himself in Hades, being tormented in "flames" (Luke 16:23–24). He is given access to the goings-on in heaven, and sees the great Jewish patriarch, Father Abraham, with Lazarus by his side. Now the

3. Both Gadenz, *Gospel of Luke*, 287, and Green, *Gospel of Luke*, 605, think the depiction of the rich man resembles the reported extravagance of kings in Jesus' time: Herod Antipas and Agrippa, respectively. What if a subtext of this parable is a critique of the royal lifestyles in the neighborhood, including that of the Herodian family that arrested and murdered John the Baptist?

4. Gadenz, *Gospel of Luke*, 287.

5. Levine, *Short Stories of Jesus*, 277.

6. Stephanie Buckhannon Crowder, "Gospel of Luke," in Blount, *True to Our Native Land*, 176, directly connects the early death of Lazarus to the indifferent behavior of the rich man: "The reader cannot help but ask whether the rich man is a 'murderer' because he did nothing to hep Lazarus in his destitute state . . . The rich man's refusal to provide food for Lazarus, to give him medical attention, or to offer him shelter put Lazarus in a . . . state that contributed to Lazarus' demise and subsequent death."

rich man is the one who seeks mercy from Lazarus, just a bit of mercy to cool the heat of the flames.[7] But again there is no mercy on offer. Abraham tells the rich man that he had his chance during his lifetime, and he missed it (Luke 16:25). There are no more chances. Notice that the rich man can identify Lazarus by name (Luke 16:24)—as Levine so powerfully states: "That knowledge condemns him."[8] The rich man cannot say that he did not know there was a man at his gate who needed help, because he knew him, *by name.*

The rich man's attention turns to his presumably just-as-much-in-trouble brothers. He wants them to be warned. Send Lazarus to them before it is too late (Luke 16:27–28). But Abraham says they have plenty of warning, just like the rich man did—they have the law and the prophets (Luke 16:29). But the man knows that they are not listening, and that if their current course continues, they too will be doomed. He begs Abraham to send Lazarus from the dead to warn them (Luke 16:30). The kicker final line is this: "If they do not listen to Moses and the prophets, neither will they be convinced if someone rises from the dead" (Luke 16:31).

We have noted the various evasion strategies that Christians have developed through the centuries to avoid listening to Jesus and obeying what he taught. This passage offers a good example. Christians have found it very difficult to accept that Jesus might be teaching that eternal judgment could be based on a lifestyle of extravagant luxurious living combined with indifference to the poor. The idea that this behavioral pattern matters *that much* to Jesus is simply incomprehensible. And so we find various ways to avoid reading this passage, or at least reading it as if Jesus meant what he said.

Many modern Christians shy away from discussing eternal judgment in any case. And on occasions where Christians are willing to talk about eternal judgment, about heaven and hell, many have followed a different paradigm, teaching that judgment is based on right belief. If we have opened that paradigm up a bit to consider behavioral criteria as well, our list of relevant behaviors has rarely included the handling of money and treatment of the poor.

But this theme is consistent with Jesus. We have seen it multiple times already. Jesus has warned about storing up treasures on earth (Matt 6:19). Treasures in heaven (Matt 6:20) are what God cares about. These latter

7. Green, *Gospel of Luke*, 608, sees the rich man as having learned nothing from his experience, as he continues to make demands from Hades (!), including wanting to use the dead Lazarus as his errand boy.

8. Levine, *Short Stories of Jesus*, 278.

treasures are accrued by giving alms to the poor and otherwise investing in God's reign of justice (Matt 6:33). Jesus has proclaimed a kingdom of God (Mark 1:14–15) and challenged all earthly kingdoms. He has blessed the poor (Luke 6:20) and warned the rich of a coming judgment (Luke 6:24). He has invited a rich young man to sell all and follow him (Mark 10:17–22), then warned of the spiritual dangers of riches (Mark 10:23–27). He has encouraged almsgiving, though without show (Matt 6:2–4). He has taught economic simplicity and to trust in God for enough (Matt 6:25–32). He has urged giving to those who ask (Matt 5:42). He has warned through the parable of the rich fool who tears down his too-small barns rather than give his excess crop to the poor (Luke 12:13–21). He has said that one cannot serve both God and Mammon (Matt 6:24, Luke 16:13).

Levine shows that Jesus is not original in these themes. Certainly, there are plenty of teachings scattered in "Moses and the prophets." Writings of more recent vintage near the time of Jesus help us see the theme. Consider this text, which Levine finds in the intertestamental book of Tobit 4:

> Give alms according to your circumstances, my son, and do not turn your face away from anyone who is poor. Then the face of God will not be turned away from you. Act according to what you have, my son. If you have much, give alms from it; if you have little, give alms in accordance with what you have. Do not be afraid, my son, to give alms. You will be laying up a good treasure for yourself against a day of need. For almsgiving delivers from death and keeps you from going into the darkness. Indeed, almsgiving, for all who practice it, is an excellent offering in the presence of the Most High. (Tob 4:7–11)

The parable of the rich man and Lazarus does not depart from OT or intertestamental teachings on charity and kindness to the poor. Indeed, it could be understood to be a commentary on it. The rich man did not give alms to poor Lazarus. He turned his face away. He owned much but did not give in accordance with what he had. He did not lay up a good treasure for himself. Because he did not give alms, he was not delivered from death, and not kept from going into a very dark, warm place called Hades.

We will not engage any more teachings of Jesus on wealth, luxury, alms, or indifference to the poor. This is the culminating text in Luke, and in the Gospels. It packs such a powerful punch that Christians have been trying to hide from it for millennia.

We have Moses and the prophets teaching us these things. We also have one who lived, who taught this exceedingly clear parable, who died on a Roman cross, and who rose from the dead. It seems that many of us supposed followers of Jesus "do not listen to Moses and the prophets, neither [are we] convinced even if someone rises from the dead" (Matt 6:24).

32

The Widow Who Demands Justice

And will not God grant justice to his chosen ones who cry to him day and night? Will he delay long in helping them? I tell you, he will quickly grant justice to them. And yet, when the Son of Man comes, will he find faith on earth?

—LUKE 18:7–8

Text: Luke 18:1–8

THIS PASSAGE MAY OFFER the best example of a case in which a Gospel writer's summary of the meaning of a parable may distract from what Jesus was trying to teach. Luke says this is a parable about "praying always and not losing heart" (Luke 18:1) or becoming discouraged. But this is only one possible reading of the parable's meaning. The parable of the "importunate widow" or "the unjust judge" is also a parable about human justice, right here and now. Because Christians don't often think of Jesus teaching directly about justice, this parable is especially important. We need direct evidence that Jesus noticed and cared about the human struggle for justice. That is present here.

We learn of a local judge in an unnamed city. His character is strikingly described as not fearing God and not respecting people (Luke 18:2). This is exactly the opposite of the kind of person that Israel wanted in judicial authority—or really, that anyone who cares about justice should want in a position of authority. NT scholar Joel Green writes, "Within this world, the world of Luke, neither fearing God nor having regard for persons signified one's thorough wickedness."[1]

Judges need to respect people because they have grave and unique responsibilities in relation to human well-being. In any justice system, much depends on the moral compass and ethical vision of judges. At least from a Jewish or Christian perspective, judges need to fear God so that they recognize that they too are under authority, that they too will be held accountable for their own conduct before the God who is watching them.

That was Israel's understanding (cf. 2 Chr 19:7), and for many centuries the understanding of the "ministerial" authority in Christian countries as well. Public authorities exist to serve people and the community under the ultimate watchful authority of God (cf. Rom 13:1–7)—not a god we make in our own image, but the true God whose law and will transcend culture and self-interest and challenge everyone to meet the standard of justice.[2]

But this judge, completely violating biblical expectations of justice and the role of the judge, has none of that—no respect for God, no fear of people. Still, people have no choice but to come to him for justice. Our first customer today is a widow who is in some kind of legal dispute. "In that city there was a widow who kept coming to him and saying, 'Grant me justice against my opponent'" (Luke 18:3; Gk: *antidikos*). This Greek term generally means opponent or adversary in a legal matter. The word translated justice here (Gk: *ekdikeō*) means to execute right or justice, and can carry the connotation of avenging, or obtaining vengeance.[3] We know three things in one sentence: the plaintiff is a widow, she seeks justice against an adversary in a legal matter, and she comes to the judge repeatedly.

Jewish listeners would immediately hear echoes of the numerous teachings in the Law and the Prophets about the special vulnerability of widows—along with orphans, aliens, and strangers, people who generally lacked social power—and the obligation to attend especially to their needs (Exod 22:22; Deut 10:18; Isa 1:17; Jer 22:3, etc.). They might also think

---

1. Green, *Gospel of Luke*, 639.

2. What to make of this crucial biblical concept in modern, religiously pluralistic societies is a complex matter that I have taken up in *Defending Democracy from its Christian Enemies*.

3. Levine, *Short Stories of Jesus*, 242–43. Levine sees the widow as not just persistent, and not just demanding justice, but quite possibly on a quest for vengeance into which she is trying to enlist a "co-opted judge."

about the various plucky widows found in stories in the Hebrew Bible, such as Naomi and Ruth.[4]

The widow in this story appears to be harassed and harassing. She badgers the indifferent judge with constant visits, and in the end, she "wears him out" (Luke 18:5; Gk: *hypōpiazō*), until he grants her request. Amy-Jill Levine argues that the NRSV is far too bland and polite here. A better translation of what the judge fears—sometimes showing up in footnotes—is "she will beat me up," or "strike me in the face," or "give me a black eye."[5] The judge appears to fear being struck by the widow who is demanding justice. Whether that fear is realistic is not stated. Close reading of the Greek here makes the widow a tougher and more formidable character than our stereotypes often allow. Ultimately, the judge reluctantly grants her request, perhaps for his own protection.

In Luke, Jesus makes this a parable to encourage persistence in prayer. Believers are to be like the "importunate" (desperate, pleading) widow, to be the kind of people who pray day and night for God's justice to prevail. Jesus wonders at the end of his parable whether faith will hold out till the end, till he returns: "When the Son of Man comes, will he find faith on earth?" (Luke 18:8).

In this parable, we find a classic "lesser to greater" or "how much more" (*qal vahomer*) argument.[6] If even a heartless, careless, unjust judge will ultimately respond to a widow's persistent "prayers" for justice, how much more will a good and loving God respond to our prayers? We should not read the judge as being anything like God, but as an all-too-human object lesson.

The final line of the parable also shows Jesus' awareness that persistent injustice is a threat to faith in God. That is one of the most important things about this parable. The Jesus that we meet in the Gospels speaks from the margins, from below. He speaks of a coming kingdom, one of whose

---

4. Levine, *Short Stories of Jesus*, 239–40. In JANT, 152, Levine notes: "Biblical tradition offers images of widows ranging from poor, under divine protection, and requiring community support (e.g., Deut 27:19), to wealthy, stealthy, and deathly (e.g., Abigail, Judith, perhaps Jael). Levine seems to read this widow under the latter category.

5. Levine, *Short Stories of Jesus*, 254. Green, *Gospel of Luke*, 641: "The language Luke uses is startling, perhaps even humorous, borrowed as it is from the boxing ring, for it invokes the image of the almighty, fearless macho judge cornered and slugged by the least powerful in society." Like Levine, Green does not believe the NRSV's weaker translation to be the best one. "Give a black eye" is better!

6. Green, *Gospel of Luke*, 637.

characteristics will be justice—at last, justice. He looks up, up, up at the social order, the human hierarchy, those above, with their money, power, and indifference to everyone else. He sees their characteristic indifference to those below them.

Jesus knows that for the beaten down ones of this world, who cry for a justice that their hearts know is due them, and that the Scriptures themselves say is God's will, the grinding reality of injustice can indeed be a threat not just to their morale but to their faith in God. Think of the enslaved Jewish people crying for justice for four hundred years, and the enslaved African American people crying for justice for 250 years in what became the United States of America. Surely many lost their faith along the way. Jesus is asking his followers not to lose faith as they cry out for justice.[7]

This brief, powerful story reveals the dynamics of garden-variety injustice in the world, the desperate efforts some must undertake to get basic justice needs met, and the grinding challenge of injustice to faith. God's long silences in the face of our cries for justice do indeed threaten faith in God. NT scholar Pablo Gadenz notes that this story "reflects the lived tension between the promise of prompt justice and the experience of delay in God's response to prayer."[8] This became very clear to me in reading Jewish post-Holocaust theology. I heard it again while writing this chapter and sitting with a child of Holocaust survivors.

In the end we might be reminded of Jesus' own sad cry of dereliction: "My God, my God, why have you forsaken me?" (Matt 27:46). This Jesus understands what it is like to believe in a God of justice in an unjust world. In this way, like so many others, he understands us—while, in the end, offering a paradigm both of faith and of faithfulness.

7. Crowder, "Gospel of Luke," in Blount, *True to Our Native Land*, 178, puts it this way: "Luke shows how important it is that people initiate the call for justice. When we call, God answers. When we cry out, God responds. When we beg and implore God to come and see about us, God comes to make it all right." And yet, of course, it is often a very long wait.

8. Gadenz, *Gospel of Luke*, 302.

33

The Pharisee and the Tax Collector

I tell you, this man went down to his home justified rather than the other, for all who exalt themselves will be humbled, but all who humble themselves will be exalted.

—*LUKE 18:14*

Text: Luke 18:9–14

CONCERN ABOUT AN ANTI-JEWISH reading of the New Testament certainly finds a reasonable target with this parable that invites a reading unfavorably comparing a pious Pharisee with a repentant tax collector. While there are numerous texts that make Pharisees into the antagonists of Jesus in the name of righteousness, this one is especially memorable. Christians who care about not reinforcing anti-Jewish readings of Scripture need to take special care with this text. But exactly what to make of it, considering that concern, is not easily determined.

Luke sets the interpretation of the parable in advance: "He also told this parable to some who trusted in themselves that they were righteous and regarded others with contempt" (Luke 18:9). Luke tells us that this is a parable about self-righteousness, religious pride, and contempt for those deemed spiritually inferior. Remembering that Jesus' sayings circulated orally and perhaps eventually in written form before they were edited into the four Gospels, we are reminded that the parable, on the one hand, and the interpretation of it offered by Luke, are in principle separable. That should be kept in mind. This would make Luke 18:9 and 18:14 brackets that Luke has placed around Jesus' brief parable, found in Luke 18:10–13.

Turning to the parable itself: in a brilliant bit of storytelling, the parable offers a split screen of two men at the temple praying.

The Pharisee stands by himself and prays (Luke 18:11–12), and it is his prayer that is described first. The tax collector stands far off, won't even look up to heaven, and beats his breast in contrition (Luke 18:13). The starkly differentiated social status of Pharisees and tax collectors in Jesus' time was clear, and it is subtly reinforced by the way the tax collector postures his body and in how he stands much farther away from the center of activity in the temple.[1]

The Pharisee prays *by himself*, indeed one could translate this as "to himself."[2] If the latter is the reading, his prayer could be read as one of those internal monologues that in the Gospel of Luke always means spiritual obliviousness. The tax collector also prays alone, but clearly to God.

The Pharisee's prayer reads like self-congratulation. He is offering thanks to God, but for his own goodness, by contrast with the sinfulness of "other people" (Luke 18:11). Joel Green writes: "The Pharisee's prayer begins like a thanksgiving psalm, but . . . for God's acts, the Pharisee has substituted his own."[3] The tax collector's prayer, on the other hand, is a simple contrite petition for forgiveness, a sinner praying for mercy. Perhaps he is deeply sorry for his misdeeds as a tax collector serving the Romans and likely extorting payments from his own people.[4]

The Pharisee appears to be looking down and around himself at others he believes are spiritual inferiors. The tax collector appears to be looking only at his wretched self, and his gestures of lowering his eyes and beating his breast symbolize "humility and shame."[5]

1. Green, *Gospel of Luke*, 646–47.
2. Gadenz, *Gospel of Luke*, 303, translates this as "to himself." It's about how a preposition (*pros*) is translated, and either meaning is possible. Green, *Gospel of Luke*, 648, disagrees.
3. Green, *Gospel of Luke*, 648.
4. Green, *Gospel of Luke*, 178–79.
5. Green, *Gospel of Luke*, 649.

The Pharisee claims credit for his own disciplined spiritual practices, which are indeed exemplary and go beyond the norm.[6] The tax collector claims no goodness and asks for mercy.

Luke has Jesus end his parable this way: the Pharisee receives no credit from God because he has exalted himself. The tax collector, having humbled himself, goes home right with God.[7]

Christians for centuries were taught to see the Pharisee as the prototype of legalistic self-righteousness, and the tax collector as the prototype of an abject sinner saved by grace. The latter was a special favorite for Protestant revivalists, and in general, the evangelical tradition.

We need to do better. Here are some ideas for doing so.

Jesus is making a very common move in his ministry, reversing good/bad, honor/shame, top/bottom polarities. He delights in poking such expectations in the eye.

In this case, Jewish readers would expect that the Pharisee would be honored, the tax collector scorned. Pharisees deserved and were treated with honor because of their love of God, seriousness about God's covenant, and thoughtful teaching of God's people.[8]

Tax collectors, on the other hand, deserved and were treated with scorn because they were employed collecting taxes for a foreign occupying power, often raking off quite a nice profit for themselves and living in luxury.[9]

The same Jesus who makes priests/Levites the surprise bad guys and a Samaritan the hero of his crucial illustration about the meaning of love of neighbor (Luke 10:25–37), here picks a tax collector as his religious hero and a Pharisee as his counterexample. This does not have to mean a blanket

6. Gadenz, *Gospel of Luke*, 304.

7. Levine, *Short Stories of Jesus,* 208–10, offers a quite contrary interpretation, which is signaled by her translation of Luke 18:14a: "This one is justified, alongside that one." She reads Jesus as honoring the Pharisee's goodness, with his good deeds being credited to the unrighteous tax collector who was in the temple with him that day. This is such an unfamiliar interpretation it is hard to know what to make of it. It does not appear to be what Luke makes of the parable, and Levine says it is really Luke who is responsible for historic Christian misinterpretation of the story: "Luke leads us into . . . temptation by appending the floating saying" (208) that those who exalt themselves will be humbled and those who humble themselves will be exalted. Instead, this story is about "the tax collector's ability to tap into the merit of the Pharisee and the encompassing, communal grace of the Temple system" (211).

8. Levine, *Short Stories of Jesus,* 191.

9. Levine, *Short Stories of Jesus,* 188.

negative judgment on all Pharisees, priests, or Levites, but instead a strikingly memorable way of talking about how God's kingdom works.

Whenever any of us think that we have spiritually and morally arrived, it is then that we are in the greatest spiritual and moral trouble. Real humility, awareness of our sinfulness, sensitivity to our spiritual and moral weaknesses and our shortcomings, these are the attitudes of heart that God asks of us.

We need to watch out especially when we begin comparing ourselves favorably (or, for that matter, unfavorably) with other people. "God, I thank you that I am not like other people" (Luke 18:11) is a dangerous way to begin a prayer. Any of us can arrive here. But it is particularly the besetting sin of religious people, more than of the irreligious. And some people become irreligious because they have been looked upon with contempt by the religious, one too many times.

The posture of the tax collector is entirely *coram deo* (before the sight of God)—he is looking at God alone, and he knows God is looking at him. He is not comparing himself with anyone else, whether favorably or unfavorably. This is between him and God. This reminds of Jesus' teaching about attending to the plank in our own eye and not judging or condemning others (Matt 7:1–5).

Jesus sets up this parable as a moment in time. The tax collector is caught in the act of repentance. Presumably this is a real moment of contrition and repentance, and it doesn't happen to him every day. But if he is truly repenting, he will now need to change. Like Zacchaeus, he will need to make right what he did wrong and start on a new path.

Jesus wants life change; he wants people to start on a new way of life. If the tax collector keeps doing what he is doing and keeps showing up at the temple each week praying this same prayer, something has gone wrong. As Amy-Jill Levine puts it, "Acknowledging sin and asking for mercy are both commendable actions, but if they are not accompanied by a resolve to stop sinning, they prompt cheap grace."[10]

But let's say the tax collector does change. Let's say he changes so much that he gives his unjust earnings away like Zacchaeus and starts following Jesus around as one of his disciples. What is to prevent him from then becoming proud of how much he has changed? How does he keep from heading down the path of spiritual self-righteousness? Isn't this the

---

10. Levine, *Short Stories of Jesus*, 189. The phrase "cheap grace" is one of Bonhoeffer's most famous. It is borrowed here by Levine.

besetting danger of religious conversion—that the broken sinner eventually graduates over time to become the proud religious person looking down on other people? Levine and Green both suggest that this parable may in fact be directed at Jesus' own followers, who were (and are) vulnerable to precisely this problem.[11]

What we want for the tax collector is what we should want for ourselves. Deep repentance when that is needed, life changes that are real and lasting, but never a turn toward becoming an obnoxiously self-righteous religious person. It is the combination of humility and a way of life morally pleasing to God that should be our goal. Not one or the other. It is contrition plus spiritual and moral growth, plus more contrition, plus more growth, in a cycle of moral and spiritual health that lasts a lifetime.

11. Levine, *Short Stories of Jesus*, 187; Green, *Gospel of Luke*, 646.

PART FOUR

John

34

The Woman at the Well

Many Samaritans from that city believed in him because of the woman's testimony, "He told me everything I have ever done." So when the Samaritans came to him, they asked him to stay with them, and he stayed there two days. And many more believed because of his word.

—JOHN 4:39–41

Text: John 4:1–42

WE HAVE ALREADY NOTED the historic tension between Samaritans and Jews (ch. 26).[1] Despite that tension, anyone regularly transiting between Galilee and Judea "had to go through Samaria" (John 4:4)—at least, if they were in any kind of hurry, for there was an alternative, much longer route. Not every trip that Jesus made through Samaria was a happy one. We learn in Luke 9:51–56 that one time a Samaritan village did not show hospitality to Jesus when he traversed the area. This incited James and John, who clearly had their nickname Sons of Thunder (Mark 3:17) for a reason, to want to call down fire from heaven, which Jesus declined.

---

1. This history of religious-ethnic-national intertwining and hostility is described helpfully by Morris, *Gospel According to John*, 226–27.

In this story, Jesus' humanity is humbly revealed. He sits by a well at noon, because he is tired and thirsty. A Samaritan woman comes to the well, and Jesus asks her for a drink. Some commentators have thought it odd that the woman came at the peak of the day's heat to this well. Perhaps she did so to avoid others. This was a traditional interpretation, assuming the woman had a bad reputation or damaged relations with other women.[2] (See below for a challenge to that assumption.) In any case, it appears to be just the two of them in the midday sun at Jacob's well.[3]

The woman is surprised that Jesus initiates a conversation with her and is willing to drink from anything that she had handled. The Gospel narrator discusses the latter in this way: "Jews do not share things in common with Samaritans" (John 4:9). The Greek term rendered here as "share things in common" is the word *sugchraomai.* It can also be rendered as "associate with," "have dealings with," or "use together." The Jews did not associate, deal with, share things, or use the same things as Samaritans, period. (It is interesting, then, that Jesus' disciples were able to go and buy lunch in Samaria. Perhaps the barrier was not so airtight.)

Most commentators suggest that it was indeed a surprise that a Jewish man like Jesus would speak to a Samaritan woman—both because she was a woman, and because she was a Samaritan. Adele Reinhartz, in the *Jewish Annotated New Testament,* claims that it was not uncommon or forbidden at the time for Jewish men to speak with women, but also cites Second Temple era texts that warn men against doing so (cf. Sir 9:1–9).[4] This may parallel a situation today in conservative Christianity in which some, especially pastors, set very tight boundaries on their contacts with people of the opposite sex, while others do not.

In any case, from the first moment of this story we have gender, religious, and ethnic divisions between the two, which are rapidly being overcome by Jesus and the unnamed woman.

There are some interesting comparisons and contrasts between this story and the one in John 3 involving Nicodemus. Both have private conversations with Jesus, and both have great trouble understanding the metaphorical language that Jesus uses. Nicodemus can't understand how a

2. Morris, *Gospel of John,* 228.

3. The location is a bit problematic geographically, but overall, the point is that the story "takes place in territory once inhabited by the patriarchs," and is a reminder that "Samaritans and Jews share a common ancestry." Thompson, *John,* 98.

4. Adele Reinhartz, notes to "The Gospel According to John," in JANT, 184.

grown person can slip back into his mother's womb and be born again, but "born again" is a spiritual metaphor. The Samaritan woman can't understand how Jesus can get "living water" from Jacob's well without a bucket (John 4:11), but living water is a spiritual metaphor. Nicodemus is a male leader of the Jewish people, while, as the *Women's Bible Commentary* says, this person at the well is "a female member of an enemy people."[5] Nicodemus comes to Jesus under the cover of night, the woman at the well speaks to him in broad daylight. NT scholar Love Lazarus Secrest suggests that comparing the two stories places the Samaritan woman in a far better light than Nicodemus.[6]

When the woman at the well hears about the living, everlastingly satisfying "water" that Jesus offers, she wants some, so that she will never have to come back to the well in the heat of the day (John 4:15). She is missing the deep metaphorical significance of water in the Jewish tradition, but as NT scholar Marianne Meye Thompson points out, "that scriptural background was not fully available to the Samaritan woman," as the Samaritans recognized only the Pentateuch as Scripture, whereas the symbolic meanings of water are developed later in the OT.[7]

Jesus next makes what seems an off-topic comment to the woman about going and getting her husband and then coming back (John 4:16). She reveals that she has no husband. Jesus responds by referring to her five former husbands and current live-in boyfriend.

This fact has led most NT interpreters, historically male, to assume the woman's dubious sexual morality,[8] the purported scandal of which is a key part of how the story has been read. This is in fact an assumption. As NT scholar Gail O'Day points out, the woman might be caught in the levirate marriage system, having to marry dead husbands' brothers, with the last surviving brother being unwilling to marry her.[9] Perhaps she has simply been widowed and remarried several times. Secrest also points out the possibility that the woman has been divorced multiple times, against her will.[10] Maybe it was a combination of these situations. Given patriarchal power structures, women often did not have full agency over their own sexual and marital

5. Gail R. O'Day, "Gospel of John," in *Women's Bible Commentary*, 521.

6. Secrest, *Race and Rhyme*, 135.

7. Ford, *Gospel of John*, 108.

8. Morris, *Gospel According to John*, 234, takes this traditional reading.

9. O'Day, "Gospel of John," in *Women's Bible Commentary*, 521–22.

10. Secrest, *Race and Rhyme*, 133, citing the research of NT scholar Lynn Cohick.

lives.[11] Feminist interpreters are explicitly attempting to counter how the passage has been interpreted to assume the woman's supposed immorality.[12]

Due to this total stranger's supernatural knowledge of her history, the woman senses that Jesus is a prophet. Then, perhaps to deflect, or simply to explore further, she opens a classic Jew/Samaritan debate over where the right location to worship God is (John 4:19–20).

Jesus refers to the eschatological moment in which worship will happen "in spirit and truth" (John 4:23) and not in any disputed location. The woman defers such questions to the time when Messiah comes, for "he will proclaim all things to us" (John 4:25). Using the powerfully significant "I AM" language (*egō eimi*), which connects to the holy name of God in the Hebrew Bible, Jesus reveals himself to be Messiah (John 4:26).

The disciples come back with the food they have acquired—and are astonished that Jesus is talking with a Samaritan woman (John 4:27). The woman, in turn, leaves her water jar behind to go tell all her neighbors about Jesus (John 4:28–30). Jesus doesn't eat (John 4:31–38), content and fulfilled for the moment with doing his Father's work, caught up in the gravity of what is now happening.

The woman returns with her community. And then, "Many Samaritans from that city believed in him because of the woman's testimony" (John 4:39). The community offers Jesus and his disciples their hospitality, and they stay two full days before moving forward to Galilee (4:40–45). During those days, many more Samaritans listen to Jesus and come to believe in him.

Jesus chose to reveal his messianic identity to the Samaritan woman. The woman, in turn, has served as an effective evangelist, introducing Jesus to an entire community of Samaritans, many of whom have rapidly embraced him.

What are the moral lessons to be learned from this story?

Everyone is shocked that Jesus is even in this conversation with this Samaritan, this woman, this Samaritan woman, but Jesus is not shocked.

11. Thompson, *John*, 103, suggests, "The woman's repeated marriages would not have made her a more desirable candidate for marriage. That she is currently living with a man outside a legally contracted marriage indicates to some commentators her immorality but to others also her desperation. She needs the protection and support of a husband, but has settled for what she can get."

12. Ford, *Gospel of John*, 113: "[T]here is no explicit suggestion in the story of her being immoral or ashamed . . . *whatever the truth, a life shot through with disappointment, pain, and grief is suggested.*" Italics in the original.

The Gospel succeeds in this Samaritan city because Jesus chooses to sit and talk with a most unlikely person, meeting her with respect and compassion.

The woman, in turn, runs to her neighbors with the good news that a Jewish man over at Jacob's well is the promised Messiah. She has assumed a role parallel to that of John the Baptist and the disciples—she has become an evangelist for Jesus the Messiah. Meanwhile, the overall event has led to a meaningful Samaritan-Jew rapprochement. Hospitality has been extended across those tense religious and ethnic lines. Good news, indeed.

35

The Woman Facing Execution

When they kept on questioning him, he straightened up and said to them, "Let anyone among you who is without sin be the first to throw a stone at her."

—*JOHN 8:7*

Text: John 7:53—8:11

THE STORY OF THE woman facing execution on an accusation of adultery is one of the most memorable of all the texts associated with Jesus Christ. But the passage does not appear in any NT manuscript before 400 CE.[1] Where it does appear, it is sometimes placed elsewhere in John or in manuscripts of the Gospel of Luke, often after Luke 21:38. Its vocabulary does not appear to fit the Gospel of John.[2]

---

1. Secrest, *Race and Rhyme*, 156.

2. Allen Dwight Callahan, "Gospel of John," in Blount, *True to Our Native Land*, 196, notes that it contains the sole reference to scribes and elders in the Gospel. O'Day, "Gospel of John," in *Women's Bible Commentary*, 522, describes the unique difficulty this creates for interpreting the story: "While one can comment on the contents of and theology of this particular passage, one cannot really move from there to talk about how this passage fits in the larger scheme of John. John 7:53—8:11 is a story without a time or place." Its disputed place in the canon means that, especially for Protestants, it is not clear if

The reason we still find it in (most of) our Bibles, even if bracketed or footnoted, is because of its extraordinary power. The church has simply loved this story too much to keep it out of our collective memory of Jesus. "Its witness coheres theologically and historically with the canonical portrait of Jesus."[3] And so, we keep telling the story, and we keep learning from it and being formed by it.

Scribes and Pharisees bring to Jesus a woman who (allegedly) has been caught in the act of adultery. They make her stand in front of "all of them," a presumably massive early morning crowd at the temple that has come to hear Jesus teach. The religious leaders then refer Jesus to the command that adulterers be executed (Lev 20:10, Deut 22:22). They ask for his comment on the matter.

At one level, this is a legal case, and Jesus is being asked to render a legal judgment. In the presence of a massive crowd of onlookers of every type, together with Jewish religious authorities—scribes, Pharisees, temple officials—undoubtedly accompanied by nearby Roman soldiers, whose ranks were beefed up during Passover week each year—Jesus is asked to rule on a capital case. Should this woman die?

Torah required two or three eyewitnesses for execution (Deut 17:6). Presumably the teachers bringing the woman to Jesus have also brought the requisite eyewitnesses alleging adultery. This does not appear to be a matter of a husband's jealous suspicion but of eyewitness testimony to adultery. On the other hand, it is not impossible that the accusation is false. Just because the woman is accused does not mean she is guilty.

Commentators often like to point out the gendered injustice of this situation, saying things like "it takes two to commit adultery," so where is the man? Good question. Under Jewish Law, if the man and the woman involved here were both married to other people, both are guilty of committing adultery and both should be brought to Jesus for a ruling. But if the man was not married while the woman was, technically she would have been the only one who committed adultery.[4]

By the first century, it appears that executions imposed by Jewish authorities were very rare. Jewish self-rule was limited under Roman

---

this story actually is "in" the New Testament. Some commentaries simply do not treat it.

3. Thompson, *John*, 179.

4. Thompson, *John*, 180: "The scribes and Pharisees bring only one of the guilty parties, letting the man off the hook."

occupation in Judea, though some judicial authority was reserved to the Sanhedrin.

But it should be noted that this is not in fact a judicial setting. There has been no convening of a proper authority, no trial, no interrogation of witnesses, nothing like that. A lone woman is surrounded by a group of men who, at the very least, want to use her case to test Jesus (John 8:6) and who may well believe that she deserves to die.

"They said this to test him, so that they might have some charge to bring against him" (John 8:6).

This is indeed a test for Jesus, one of several times in the Gospels when Jesus' adversaries think they might have him boxed in, caught in a no-win situation.

If Jesus refuses to support enforcing the death penalty provision of Torah for adultery, he can be made to look like a lawless rebel against God. But if he supports enforcing this mandate in Torah, his reputation for mercy will be destroyed along with the woman's life.

Also, the law of the Roman occupiers did not permit executions for adultery.[5] Therefore, in relation to Rome, if Jesus refuses to support the woman's execution, he could be seen as abandoning Torah to knuckle under to illegitimate pagan authority. But if he flaunted that authority by supporting her on-the-spot execution in the name of Moses, this could have been the spark for an uprising.[6]

Readers have been so fascinated by this next move:

"Jesus bent down and wrote with his finger on the ground. When they kept on questioning him, he straightened up and said to them, 'Let anyone among you who is without sin be the first to throw a stone at her.' And once again he bent down and wrote on the ground" (John 8:6–8).

There are many theories as to why Jesus is writing on the ground, and what he is writing.[7] Perhaps he is writing out his verdict, as Roman judges did before reading them aloud. Perhaps he is slowing down the mob by breaking into their rage with his deliberative silence. Perhaps with supernatural knowledge Jesus is writing down some of the sins of the people who have brought the woman to him. Among other things, I think he is

---

5. Reinhartz, in JANT, 193.

6. Ford, *Gospel of John*, 175.

7. Thompson, *John*, 180, notes that "the tablets of the law [were] written by the finger of God" (Deut 9:10). Perhaps this is an allusion to the writing of the Law, with Jesus compared to Moses as lawgiver or as authoritative interpreter of Torah.

protecting the woman's dignity by refusing to look at her in her state of terror. She might also have been naked or immodestly covered.[8]

His words strike with brutal, unmistakable power, in a formulation so unforgettable that it has inscribed itself in the memory of Bible readers for two millennia: *Let him who is without sin cast the first stone* (John 8:7).[9]

This move was entirely novel on Jesus' part. There had been no idea like it in OT Law. It is entirely subversive to any legal system. Judging crime has nothing to do with the virtue of the jurors, judges, jailers, or anyone else involved in the system. If no one guilty of sin can participate in legal cases or law enforcement, then there can be no legal cases or law enforcement.

But in this situation, that is precisely what Jesus is requiring of all those men. Only after they take an inventory of their own lives are they released to hurl their missiles at the temple of the woman in the temple of the Lord. Only once each man has concluded that he is innocent of all sins is he free to execute.

Maybe there was something fishy about the whole deal, and Jesus had sniffed it out. Perhaps the whole thing was a setup against the woman, as in the story of Susanna, falsely accused of adultery in Daniel 13, another late text which is in the Catholic but not the Protestant Bible.[10]

Most will remember how this story ends. No one throws a stone. "They went away, one by one, beginning with the elders" (John 8:9).

The oldest have the longest memories. They have had time to develop greater self-awareness. And in Jewish culture they would have understood that they had the greatest communal responsibility.[11]

So, as if in a procession, they just walked away, one by one. Jesus was left with the woman. According to the story, literally everyone else had left.

Only now, with the crowd gone, does Jesus straighten up and look directly in the eyes of the woman whose life he has saved. His tenderness is palpable. We picture her trembling uncontrollably with those near-miss trembles that come when death has passed very close by.

---

8. Secrest, *Race and Rhyme*, 161.

9. The male singular pronoun is the most appropriate here.

10. In the Protestant Bible, the book of Daniel ends with chapter 12. Secrest, *Race and Rhyme*, 156–61, makes the potential Susanna parallel central to her interpretation, suggesting that the intertextuality of the two stories is intentional. And, just as the accusation against Susanna was false, so, Secrest suggests that this accusation is also false (163).

11. Callahan, "Gospel of John," in Blount, *True to Our Native Land*, 196, suggests the interpretation that "Jesus had no takers because the erstwhile stone-throwers were former paramours. And everyone knew it."

Jesus asks her, "Woman, where are they? Has no one condemned you?"

She says, "No one, sir."

Jesus says, "Neither do I condemn you. Go your way, and from now on do not sin again."

And that is how the story ends (John 8:10–11).

What do we make of this story? What is its moral teaching?

In John 3 Jesus says that he did not come to condemn the world but to save it. Here Jesus enacts that commitment in real time, with a woman's life at stake.

Notice that Jesus does not demand a statement of repentance from the woman. He enacts no penalty upon her whatsoever. He offers mercy, with clear direction for living, in perfect harmony.

Human beings, including Christians, don't do this kind of thing very well. Either we judge people mercilessly or we slide into casual normless relativism in which anything goes. We err on the side of judgment, or we err on the side of grace, or we ping-pong back and forth without any consistency. This happens within our own souls, in our families, churches, and societies.

Legalism has its grave costs. But so does the collapse of moral standards. Jesus seems to be the only one who has ever gotten the balance exactly right. Jesus is the only one who knows fully, completely, and without bias what is going on in the human heart. Jesus puts it all together—knowledge, truth, holiness, justice, grace. Love Lazarus Secrest writes: "Jesus is the one trusted to judge with right judgment, who judges with the insight of God in contrast to human decisions that focus on appearances. Likewise, may we all seek the mind of Christ."[12]

12. Secrest, *Race and Rhyme*, 164.

36

Love One Another

I give you a new commandment, that you love one another . . . By this everyone will know that you are my disciples, if you have love for one another.

—JOHN 13:34–35

This is my commandment, that you love one another as I have loved you.

—JOHN 15:12

Texts: John 13:31–35, 15:12–17

THE GOSPEL OF JOHN offers less explicit moral teaching than the other three Gospels. That is why we have so few selections from John in this book. However, here are two texts in Jesus' famous "farewell discourse" in John that do offer a singular moral teaching: *love one another*.

It is important to situate this teaching in its precise context. It is the night of the Last Supper. Jesus is deeply troubled in his spirit (John 13:21). Not only is he soon to die, but he knows that one of his inner twelve disciples will be his betrayer unto death. Jesus gives Judas Iscariot the very last morsel of food he will ever eat with his Master, and then Judas goes out into the night to betray him (John 13:21–30).

Jesus now begins saying goodbye to his disciples. He is about to be "glorified," through going willingly to his gruesome death, that classic paradox of the cross. His passion is now beginning. "I am with you only a little longer. You will look for me . . . but where I am going, you cannot come" (John 13:32–33).

It is at this precise moment that he turns to his remaining eleven and offers them what he describes as a "new commandment." The Greek here is *entolē*, which in the Septuagint translates the Hebrew *mitzvah*— "commandment" is the right English word. This is not a guideline or suggestion or even a rule—it is a *commandment*.

But what is new about it? Love of neighbor was already commanded in Torah (Lev 19:18), as we have seen (ch. 26).

Adele Reinhartz, in the *Jewish Annotated New Testament,* joins others in claiming that "in the context of this Gospel [love] has a narrower meaning referring to the love among the believers, which is not extended to unbelievers."[1]

That implication seems clear also in the repeat version of the commandment, found in John 15. The commandment is set up this way: God the Father has loved Jesus the Son, who in turn has abided in the Father's love, and with that love has loved the disciples (John 15:9–10).

Jesus is now leaving, but the love that bound him with the Father and with the disciples must not be allowed to leave as he leaves. The disciples are now to love each other in the same way that Jesus has loved them (John 15:12). They are his friends, and they are to be friends to each other. Just as he lays down his life for them, they are to do so for each other (John 15:14–15). While the world will hate them, as it has hated Jesus (John 15:18–21), they will gain strength by the love they have received from Jesus and now share with each other. Their unity in love will be the sign to the world of who they are, and Whose they are. The richness of the intimacy between Jesus and his disciples, the centrality and inexhaustibility of the love that binds them, and their promotion from "servants" to friends, are all remarkable features of this passage.

While the categorical claim may be too strong that in John Jesus teaches love only for fellow believers and not for unbelievers, it certainly seems clear from close study that this is a command directed within the

---

1. Reinhartz, in JANT, 206.

faith community, a community that sees itself in the sharpest distinction from the hostile world around it. But does this make John's moral vision inferior to that of the other Gospels?

Gail O'Day acknowledges that in John 13/15, "[t]he commandment to love one another is essentially sectarian; its primary focus is on the life of the Christian community." But then she argues: "That focus does not provide grounds for dismissing the ethical seriousness of the commandment . . . to love one another may be the most difficult thing Jesus could have asked."[2] She also celebrates the move beyond sacrifice toward friendship, mutuality, connectedness, and abundance that Jesus offers, especially in John 15. She writes, "The Johannine language of the fullness and abundance of love is very important for women, because a one-sided emphasis on emptying and self-denial has led many women (and some men) to subscribe to an ethos of perpetual self-sacrifice and the meaninglessness of self."[3]

But this kind of mutual love requires a certain kind of Christian community. The long history of the church demonstrates that Christian communities have ranged across an entire spectrum that can be described as highly bonded/insular/separatist at one pole all the way over to loosely connected/open/cosmopolitan at the other. H. Richard Niebuhr's categories of "Christ *against* Culture," on the one hand, and "Christ *of* Culture," on the other hand, remain helpful here.[4]

There are three other options that Niebuhr describes, but what is relevant for our purposes is that the church that Jesus is forming here, as we find it in John especially, is indeed highly bonded and insular. These believers are tightly connected to each other, are being taught a highly demanding sacrificial love ethic in relation to each other, and feel a strong and clear sense of distinction from outsiders. Perhaps, as most NT scholars surmise, the Johannine community was an embattled one that faced rejection, expulsion, and persecution. That kind of rejection often creates this kind of communal vision.

Such religious communities, however they emerge, can be described pejoratively as closed, intolerant, and hostile to the world. But, on the other hand, they can also be described positively as clear in identity, unified in vision, and bonded in community.

2. O'Day, "Gospel of John," in *Women's Bible Commentary*, 525.
3. O'Day, "Gospel of John," in *Women's Bible Commentary*, 526.
4. H. Richard Niebuhr, *Christ and Culture*.

At its worst, such versions of Christian community can become holier-than-thou, unable to learn anything from anyone else and spoiling for a fight with outsiders. But the other pole has its worst side too—Christians who are indistinguishable from the wider world, do not feel much connection to each other, and do not demonstrate that being a believer in Jesus makes any practical difference in life. Many contemporary churches are weak, diffuse, low-commitment assemblages of acquaintances and strangers.

Because humans are sinful and limited, and Christians are humans, there will never be a perfect form of Christian community. Every version of church has its problems and its risks. But still, a community of highly connected believers who truly love each other, who serve each other, who sacrifice for each other, and who do all this as an expression of their love for Jesus Christ, has a very great deal to recommend it.

Jesus taught that the very existence of such communities would help to show the world that Jesus is real and that these persons are really his disciples. As theologian David Ford writes, "Love . . . in the Christian family is to be the primary sign that we really are disciples of Jesus . . . The mission of the church is inseparable from the sort of community the church is."[5]

5. Ford, *Gospel of John*, 266.

37

May They All Be One

I ask not only on behalf of these but also on behalf of those who believe
in me through their word, that they may all be one.

—JOHN 17:20–21

Text: John 17:20–24

JOHN 17 IS OFTEN labeled as "Jesus' high-priestly prayer." This is because
he stands in the sight of God praying for his people. In this extraordinarily
profound soliloquy, Jesus first prays (John 17:1–5) that he will be glorified
in his death, in order that his Father will be glorified. Next (John 17:6–19)
Jesus prays that his followers will be protected and sanctified. And in our fo-
cal passage (John 17:20–24), Jesus prays for all generations of his followers,[1]
that they would "become completely one" (v. 23).

This is a prayer for Christian unity, the unity of all believers. Jesus
asks that the unity that he enjoys with the Father would be theirs. This is
available to the church through participating in the unity of the Godhead
(reading v. 21 as "may they also be *one in us*"). Verse 22 expands the basis
of Christian unity as relating to the "glory"—revelation of God's splendor

---

1. Morris, *Gospel According to John*, 649; Ford, *Gospel of John*, 347.

and power—that God has given Jesus. Jesus says he has passed this glory on to the disciples, for the purpose that "they may be one, as we are one."[2]

The purpose of Christian unity is described twice as evangelistic—"so that the world may believe that you have sent me" (v. 21), and "so that the world may know that you have sent me and have loved them even as you have loved me" (v. 23). But, as Marianne Meye Thompson writes, "The mission of the disciples only expresses their unity; it does not create that unity," which "exists, not because of human effort, but because of God's life-giving love for the world that is expressed through and in the mission of Jesus."[3]

The Jesus we see in John is praying to his Father for the unity of believers. That unity is possible due to the nature of God the Father's relationship with God the Son, a mystery (perhaps the universe's very highest mystery) in which those whom the Son has gathered in community participate. That relationship is understood as ineffably united, noncompetitive, mutually serving, and loving. It is part of the "glory" of Christ, and Christ has passed it forward to his followers as a sublime expression of his love for them. This unity and the love that makes it possible demonstrate God's glory and aid in the spread of belief in Jesus in the world.

On one level, this is not a "moral teaching of Jesus." Jesus is offering no moral imperatives here. This is part of a grand farewell prayer, part of a series of Jesus' last requests to God his Father before going to the cross. We are privileged to listen in on what God the Son is saying to God the Father before going to die.

But prayers also teach because they articulate earnest desire. A publicly articulated prayer teaches something about what that person considers important. If we go to church and the pastor prays that everyone present will become wealthy one day, the people learn from the pastor to value, pray for, and seek wealth. Whereas if the pastor prays that everyone who has a conflict with a sister or brother would be reconciled, the people learn to value, pray for, and seek peace.

In this way, through his prayer, Jesus is teaching the value of Christian unity. He yearns for this for his followers—that they "may become completely one" (John 17:23).[4] This certainly seems to mean that we Christians

2. Morris, *Gospel According to John*, 650, notes that in John, "true glory was to follow the path of lowly service culminating in the cross."

3. Thompson, *John*, 356.

4. Complete can also be translated "perfected." Morris, *Gospel According to John*, 651: "They already had a unity of a sort. But this unity is not regarded as being sufficient. Theirs is to be a closer unity, a 'perfected' unity."

should also desire oneness. We should want it for the reason that Jesus wanted it—because it bears a positive witness to God's nature and love in Jesus Christ and thus has the potential to draw people toward God. We should also want it because it is mandatory that we be who Jesus says we are—participants in the oneness of God the Father and the Son, and recipients of the glory that the Father gave the Son, and the Son gave us.

The Nicene Creed, formulated in 325 CE, confesses belief in "one, holy, catholic, and apostolic church." In this sense the unity of the church is a matter of conviction, a belief confessed, like belief in the resurrection, ascension, and future return of Christ. The creed does not say: "We have experienced" the oneness of the church, but instead "we believe" in it, just as we believe in the return of Christ that we have not yet experienced.

Yet this confession of faith in Christian unity also has rightly motivated numerous efforts to build such unity. Theologian David Ford notes:

> This third part of John 17 has given perhaps the main biblical impetus to the ecumenical movement within Christianity, seeking ways to be one church together . . . that movement has achieved things probably never before seen in religious history: Christian bodies with hundreds of millions of members have turned from confrontation and sometimes conflict toward conversation, frequently with collaboration, and in some cases have joined one another in full mutual recognition and sometimes even institutional unity.[5]

But sadly, Ford also notes the "innumerable splits, divisions, and conflicts" within the church—these included splits within the Johannine community itself.[6] Divisions, schisms, conflicts, controversies, sects, split-offs, firings, broken relationships, shattered congregations, doctrinal fights, hardened battle lines, and so on, have indeed characterized so many of our churches. We must acknowledge the empirical reality of Christian disunity. It contrasts so starkly with Jesus' prayer for unity here.

I wonder if Jesus, in this prayer, was already pointing obliquely but realistically to the tremendous difficulty of human beings in finding and maintaining unity. One could read his prayer something like this: O Father, I call on all the spiritual riches and mysteries and glories of our relationship with each other to fall upon these inheritors of our mission and ministry. They are going to need every bit of it, and still they will often fall short, because they are human beings in all their brokenness.

5. Ford, *Gospel of John*, 348.
6. Ford, *Gospel of John*, 348.

It may not be all that different from Jesus' request just before—that every believer would be protected and sanctified in the truth (John 17:17). Experientially, we know that many of us fall prey to temptation, lies, unholiness, and disbelief. Jesus prays for what he wants, and we need, but even his prayer is not fully answered. Think about that!

One word of warning: some of us have learned to be suspicious of calls for Christian unity amid conflicting convictions. My favorite personal example is this: when I felt called by God to oppose US-sponsored torture of detainees after the 9/11 attacks, one criticism offered by some fellow Christians was that my stand violated Christian unity. Because many Christians disagreed with me, therefore I was supposed to stand down from the fight against torture. Ha!

Arguments hushing dissent and blocking reform in the name of unity have been made in a variety of Christian settings. There is little question that the norm of Christian unity is often leveraged to silence dissent. This hushing can delay progress for marginalized people and groups within our churches and society at large. Surely this wasn't the kind of "unity" for which Jesus was praying—a lockstep conformity of all opinions, with built-in resistance to change. A mutually respectful, open-hearted, other-regarding, familial and affectionate bond of fellowship is what Jesus desired for his followers.

In sum: Jesus prays for Christian unity, and a theological conviction about the unity of the church is a historic part of Christian confession. Peace and unity are not easy, and Christians are often bitterly divided. But every time we Christians bear with one another, choose to seek peace, and remain in relationships that defy our natural human tendencies, something special is happening. At these times, we see Jesus' prayer being answered. We must never give up the quest for Christian unity.

PART FIVE

Passion Week

38

Jesus Occupies the Temple

Then he entered the Temple and began to drive out those who were
selling things there, and he said, "It is written,

'My house shall be a house of prayer,'
but you have made it a den of robbers."

—*LUKE 19:45–46*

Texts: Mark 11:15–19/Matt 21:12–13 /Luke 19:45–48 /John 2:13–22

OUR LAST THREE READINGS are situated during the last week of Jesus'
earthly life. Here we must pause to acknowledge the fraught and painful
history of the Christian Holy Week for Jewish people. There is a horrible
legacy of the holiest week of the church year being polluted by the worst
forms of antisemitism. So we should exercise extra care as we interpret
these texts.

Jesus' prophetic demonstration in the temple is one of the most famous stories in the Gospels. The Synoptic Gospels place it at the beginning
of Holy Week, which also happens to be the Jewish Passover week. Jesus
enters triumphantly into Jerusalem, where his ministry has been pointing, but never engaging, until now. Indeed, for at least Matthew and Mark,
this appears to be the Galilean prophet's first-ever visit to Jerusalem as an

adult, with all its weighty political and spiritual symbolism. The juggernaut prophet from the provinces has finally arrived in the historic capital of the Jewish people. A titanic collision is inevitable.

In Mark, Jesus' incursion into the temple takes place one day after the triumphal entry that Christians mark as Palm Sunday. That timing makes for a dramatic story. Jesus has swept into town on a wave of popular support, with crowds heralding him as representing "the coming kingdom of our ancestor David" (Mark 11:10) and offering such provocations as "blessed is the king who comes in the name of the Lord!" (Luke 19:38). These are revolutionary/messianic cries that antagonize some of the religious authorities. They demand that Jesus put a stop to them. He refuses to do so (Luke 19:39–40).

Luke offers the most compact account of what Christian tradition calls "the cleansing of the temple." Jesus goes into the temple and starts driving out the sellers and buyers there. That's it. Mark and Matthew add the detail of overturning the tables of the money changers and seats of those who sold doves. John, who places this event far earlier in Jesus' ministry (John 2:13–22), offers the more detailed and vivid imagery of Jesus "making a whip of cords" and driving all sellers and money changers out of the temple, turning over the tables, scattering their money, and so on.

In the Synoptic Gospels, Jesus accompanies his actions with quotes from these Scriptures: "My house shall be called a house of prayer." Mark adds: "for all nations," which completes the citation from Isa 56:7. In saying, "but you have made it a den of robbers," Jesus is quoting Jeremiah's diatribe at the temple (Jer 7:11). John takes the quote this way: "Stop making my Father's house a marketplace!"

Scholars have long debated what was so outrageous to Jesus about the goings-on in the temple. Interpreters can only draw inferences based on Jesus' reported actions and words. He could have been offended that the temple, the holiest place in Judaism, has become a busy, noisy place of commercial exchange.[1] It has also been argued that the court of the gentiles had been subsumed entirely by these transaction spaces, so that the temple was being prevented from serving as a house of prayer for the gentiles, the

1. Culpepper, *Matthew*, 396–97: "The temple cult in Jerusalem had become one of the largest in the Roman world. The quantity of animals and goods consumed during a festival was staggering . . . a thriving commercial enterprise [also] developed . . . A great deal of labor was required to sustain the temple's activities . . . because ancient temples, including the temple in Jerusalem, were used as banks, Jesus may have been attacking the banking operations in the temple" as well.

non-Jewish peoples who came seeking God. A holy place of prayer had become, as John puts it, a mere "marketplace," like setting up a Walmart right in front of the altar in a church.

Why, then, does Jesus call the temple a "den of robbers"? That is a powerful indictment, which goes beyond mere "marketplace" language. It has led to further examination related to the financial transactions going on in the temple.

For example, consider the money changers. In John, it is their tables that are specifically turned over. It has been argued that the money changers were cheating people as they were changing their local currency for temple currency, or even that requiring such a change of money (with associated fee) was unjust. The sellers of sacrificial animals—such as doves, the offering of the poor—may also have been exploiting their trade monopoly to extract excess profits for their transactions. This charge stings even more if we remember the great poverty of many who made their way to the temple to do what they believed God's law required of them—such as animal sacrifice.

Far-reaching examination has been made by several scholars of who exactly ran the temple and how it operated. In *Kingdom Ethics,* we cite biblical scholars such as Ched Myers, Marcus Bockmuehl, and David Garland, who argue that the temple was a highly lucrative operation run by a small elite of priests and associated officials. These few enjoyed lavish lifestyles in Jerusalem.[2] Its revenues were provided by many very impoverished people who were doing what they believed God required of them. This way of looking at it also gives a new meaning to the story of the widow giving her last penny to the temple treasury (Luke 21:1–4). Maybe Jesus was not just honoring her, he was also critiquing a religious system that would demand that last penny of her and convince her she must give it.

The Romans allowed the temple operation to continue because it helped buy off some elites in Jerusalem and kept the people pacified, in the sense that the occupying power was not blocking their religious practices. It should be noted that the Herodian dynasty, so deeply corrupt, was responsible for the vast expansion of the temple complex that was going on before and during Jesus' lifetime. The Herodian expansion of the temple was in part aimed to vouchsafe the religious credibility of this half-Jewish client dynasty. The temple was by the time of Jesus a quite impressive edifice—but

2. Gushee/Stassen, *Kingdom Ethics,* 129–31, 138.

when this was pointed out to Jesus, he promptly predicted its complete destruction (Mark 13:1–2 and parallels).

I believe that Jesus cleansed the temple as a prophetic critique offered by a brokenhearted but loyal son of Israel. While Christians have sometimes viewed his actions as utterly delegitimizing the temple, it is important to take a broader view and to avoid potential supersessionist implications.

After all, this episode is only one of many involving Jesus and the temple. Luke's Gospel goes to great lengths to situate his birth narrative around John and Elizabeth, Joseph and Mary observing temple rituals, prophets in the temple affirming Jesus' ministry, and the adolescent Jesus returning to the temple on his own initiative. During his ministry, Jesus often urges those healed of skin diseases to go to the temple to have the healing confirmed by priests. Acts describes the Jerusalem church as including three thousand priests. We know that the Jerusalem Christians, such as Jesus' brother James, still worshipped in the temple.

The Old Testament itself includes messianic prophecies that affirm the legitimacy of the temple as well as critique based on love for an institution that, like our own institutions, is subject to corruption. It is also important to note that the Qumram community had a very sharp critique of the temple, which they refused to visit. But scholars say this was mainly because they believed the current high priest to be illegitimate. In any case, this illustrates how critique of the temple was well within bounds of Jewish internal polemic of the time. While that desert community set up an alternative temple system in their community, Jesus set his face toward Jerusalem and culminated his ministry in the very temple in which he had been dedicated as a baby.

Luke's account most clearly depicts what amounts to a weeklong Jesus-movement occupation of the temple complex. After driving out the moneymaking operation, "Every day he was teaching in the Temple" (Luke 19:47).[3] Every day the religious leaders "kept looking for a way to kill him" (Luke 19:47). Every day they were thwarted because "all the people were spellbound by what they heard" (Luke 19:48).

Jesus interrupted the operations of the temple for one week. The temple became a place—the last place—where Jesus offered the good news of the kingdom of God.

---

3. Brown, "Gospel of Matthew," in Blount, *True to Our Native Land*, 111: "This act, more than any other, would have been the basis for his crucifixion. Attacks on the existing power structure, especially when it is oppressive, often bring death-dealing retaliation."

Is there a moral teaching of Jesus for us today? At least this: religious institutions are called to be the place where people are enabled to meet God. But run as they are by humans, they sometimes fail in that calling. Prophets are those who notice and proclaim that failing for what it is. Jesus functions here as the prophet par excellence when he wages his prophetic shutdown of the temple system. Quite predictably, he was dead by the weekend.

39

Paying Taxes to Caesar

Jesus said to them, "Give to Caesar the things that are Caesar's and to God the things that are God's."

—MARK 12:17

Texts: Mark 12:13–17/Matt 22:15–22 /Luke 20:20–26

WE HAVE REGULARLY ALLUDED to the fact that the Jewish people in Galilee and Judea were under the rule of Rome or Roman client kings like Herod. At the time of Jesus' ministry, Judea (including Jerusalem) was under the rule of a Roman prefect because of the earlier misrule of the Herodian Archelaus, while Rome's two other client kings in the Herodian dynasty ruled, respectively, in Galilee (Herod Antipas), and in Iturea and parts of Transjordan (Herod Philip).[1] Rome assessed an annual tax of one denarius, along with assorted other taxes.[2] Tax collectors, as we have seen, were associated in the Jewish mind with collaboration, extortion, and sinfulness.

Indeed, the whole issue of paying taxes to Rome was a very sore subject. Josephus reports a revolt in 6–7 CE under a leader from Galilee

---

1. See Martin Goodman, "Jewish History, 331 BCE–135 CE," in JANT, 583–87, for more details of this history.

2. Wills, in JANT, 52.

named Judas (cf. Acts 5:37). The revolt centered around a Roman census, an early step in the transformation of Judea into a Roman province, and the rebellion included refusing to pay taxes to Rome.[3] Judas was killed and his movement scattered.

The Roman coin introduced into Jewish lands had a depiction of the head (*eikōn*, or "image") of the empire, Caesar. That is noted explicitly by Jesus in this story. But Deut 4:16 prohibits idols in human form, and the Roman Caesars were treated as semidivine figures. Paying the tax therefore could be interpreted as violating not just Deut 4:16 but the transcendently important first commandment, which bars idolatry. A tax revolt against Rome could easily be viewed as a statement of fidelity to the one true God, the God of Israel, thus Judas the Galilean. So again here, both religion and nationalism could conspire to yield a posture by Jesus banning the payment of taxes to Rome. But such a posture was political suicide under Roman rule.

All three accounts are set in the temple during Jesus' occupation of it during Holy Week. The crowds would have been large and potentially restive, with Jewish pilgrims from not just Judea and Galilee but all over the world, and Roman soldiers milling about to keep a watchful eye on everyone.

In Matt 22/Mark 12 it is Pharisees and Herodians who question Jesus as to whether it is lawful (in Jewish terms) to pay taxes to Caesar. The Herodians are especially important because of the client dynasty relationship that the Herods had with Rome. In all three accounts the narrator tells us the question is intended to trap Jesus, to trick him into saying something that will ruin him. If he says it is lawful to pay taxes to the emperor, he could easily offend the religious and nationalist sentiments of many Jews in the crowds around him. But if he says it is unlawful, he will set himself up for immediate arrest by the nearby Roman soldiers.[4]

The setup to the question, reported in each Gospel, is flattery, which Jesus sees right through. Interestingly, his questioners offer not just a laudatory but also an insightful statement about Jesus—"Teacher, we know that you are sincere and show deference to no one, for you do not regard people with partiality but teach the way of God in accordance with truth" (Mark 12:14). Any follower of Jesus should aspire to be described in such terms.

---

3. Note interesting connections to the census described in the nativity story (Luke 2:1–7).

4. Culpepper, *Matthew*, 421–22.

Jesus' answer to his interlocutors has echoed through the ages. First, he asks them to produce "the coin used for the tax" (Matt 22:19), and they rapidly produce the denarius, which has the image of Caesar on it.[5] Then Jesus says, "Give to Caesar the things that are Caesar's, and to God the things that are God's" (Mark 12:17). With that (non) answer, according to all three Gospels, Jesus "amazed" his questioners, who give up and go away.

What was Jesus intending to teach here? Was this just a clever response, with Jesus living to see another day by refusing to offer a clear answer?

Here is an interesting detail from another story. In Luke's account of Jesus' hearing before Pilate, the Sanhedrin leaders accuse Jesus of, among other things, "forbidding us to pay taxes to Caesar" (Luke 23:2). This may mean that they, perhaps others as well, interpreted Jesus' elliptical answer as a ban on paying taxes to Caesar.

After all, what things truly belong to God, and what things truly belong to Caesar? What would Jesus likely have believed? Based on the teachings of Jesus that we have reviewed, do we have any real reason to think that Jesus believed that there is anything that does *not* belong to God, or anything that a radical God-follower owes to the Roman emperor Caesar, of all people? For Jesus, this is God's world; it is God's kingdom that is dawning; we are to serve God only. Perhaps the accusation hurled at Jesus before Pilate marked an accurate understanding of Jesus' true conviction—what belongs to God is everything, what belongs to Caesar is nothing; act accordingly.

A curious incident reported only in Matt 17:24–27 sheds more light on Jesus' attitude toward taxes:

> When they reached Capernaum, the collectors of the Temple tax came to Peter and said, "Does your teacher not pay the Temple tax?" He said, "Yes, he does." And when he came home, Jesus spoke of it first, asking, "What do you think, Simon? From whom do kings of the earth take toll or tribute? From their children or from others?" When Peter said, "From others," Jesus said to him, "Then the children are free. However, so that we do not give offense to them, go to the sea and cast a hook; take the first fish that comes up, and when you open its mouth you will find a coin; take that and give it to them for you and me."

5. Brown, "Gospel of Matthew," in Blount, *True to Our Native Land*, 112, notes: "The irony is that *they* have the coin. They are asking if it is right to participate in a system in which *they* already participate." Italics in the original.

This story seems to indicate local suspicion that Jesus and his followers did not pay the tax to support the Jerusalem temple. It appears to have been an annual half-shekel tax.[6] In any case, Peter fends off potential problems by reporting that Jesus did in fact pay the temple tax.

When the two of them discuss the matter later, however, Jesus seems to have a rather dismissive attitude toward the temple tax. It is fascinating that Jesus does not seem to draw any distinction between a temple tax and other kinds of taxes. Both are extracted by "kings of the earth" (Matt 17:25). This may shed real light on what Jesus thought about the Herodian Temple, perhaps confirming the supposition offered in the last chapter that he viewed it as just another corrupt royal project, made even more odious because of its playing on the religious heritage and hopes of the Jewish people. It was certainly yet another way for rulers to take money from burdened taxpayers. Jesus appears to declare himself and his group free of this burden but submits to paying the tax simply so as not to "give offense."

It is very important to note the ebb and flow of Christian interpretation of what was once called the "Render to Caesar" passage.

Much of the time, this text has been understood to mean just the opposite of what Jesus probably did mean. It has been read as a counsel of submission to the state. After the Roman emperor Constantine converted to Christianity in the early fourth century, and after Rome became officially Christian a few decades later, the trajectory of European and then imperial-colonial Christianity married church and state. If the Caesar is purportedly Christian, and the empire is officially Christian, surely there could be no problem (it was argued) in rendering to Caesar not just our taxes but our bodies and our loyalties. Thus the Christian kings and their religious satraps were quite happy to teach, and thus it was believed by most conventional Christians.

By setting up his answer the way that he did, however, Jesus at least drew a distinction between God's kingdom and Caesar's kingdom, between what is owed to the one and what is owed to the other. But in Christendom, this distinction was often lost. Christians failed to recognize that God is not Caesar, and Caesar is not God, and that we are citizens of another kingdom, which may demand things of us that Caesar very much resents. Those who have

---

6. Culpepper, *Matthew*, 334–35, reviews the history. The biblical basis for the tax is found in Exod 30:13 and Neh 10:32. Whether to pay the tax in the first-century Roman occupation context was disputed, though Culpepper reports that "Jews throughout the Roman Empire paid the annual tax . . . The income was sizable and the Jerusalem temple (like other temples) had vast wealth."

seen this have sometimes had to pay with their lives for their understanding of what may *not* be rendered to Caesar. What price are today's Christians willing to pay for refusing to give to Caesar what Caesar demands?

40

As You Did to the Least of These

Then the king will say to those at his right hand, "Come, you who are blessed by my Father, inherit the kingdom prepared for you from the foundation of the world, for I was hungry and you gave me food, I was thirsty and you gave me something to drink, I was a stranger and you welcomed me, I was naked and you gave me clothing, I was sick and you took care of me, I was in prison and you visited me." Then the righteous will answer him, "Lord, when was it that we saw you hungry and gave you food or thirsty and gave you something to drink? And when was it that we saw you a stranger and welcomed you or naked and gave you clothing? And when was it that we saw you sick or in prison and visited you?" And the king will answer them, "Truly I tell you, just as you did it to one of the least of these brothers and sisters of mine, you did it to me."

—MATT 25:34-40

Text: Matt 25:31-46

THIS TEXT, THE LAST block of Jesus' teaching prior to his passion, has been described by NT scholar Alan Culpepper as "the most revolutionary text in Matthew, and its social ethic is one of the most visionary in human history."[1]

It is hard to know what genre of teaching we are looking at as we encounter Jesus' words in Matt 25:31–46. Matt 25:31–46 is often called "the parable of the sheep and the goats," perhaps because it is preceded and followed by parables. But there is really nothing in our passage to signal that this is in fact a parable. It reads to me more like an unveiling of what will happen on judgment day.

The passage's imagery is rooted in the Hebrew Bible. The image of the Son of Man coming in glory, accompanied by all the angels, sitting on the throne, comes from Dan 7:13–14. Daniel has a vision in which a "son of man" (NRSV: "one like a human being") comes to earth with delegated authority. He carries divine dominion, glory, and kingship, and he acts on God's behalf.

The text centers on the later-developing idea in Jewish thought of a general resurrection of the dead, in preparation for a final judgment of all humans, as described in Dan 12:2–3. On judgment day, all nations (ethnic groups, races, peoples—*panta ta ethnē*) will be gathered before the Son of Man (Matt 25:31), who identifies himself as "king" by Matt 25:34. This judgment appears to refer to all humanity, but the matter is disputed, and we will revisit it below.

As expected in one contemporary Jewish understanding of judgment day, people are sorted into two groups, those who have merited God's positive judgment (the righteous) and those who have not (the unrighteous, or wicked). It is worth pausing over the idea that according to this teaching everyone who has ever lived is going to be judged by the same standard and the same God. It is also worth noting that for many Protestant Christians, eternal judgment has been understood to be based on belief or doctrine or conversion, not the quality of one's life. That later development was not a Jewish idea, and it is not supported by this text.

After the separation of the people into two groups, the king pronounces glorious words of blessing on those judged positively: "Come, you who are blessed by my Father, inherit the kingdom prepared for you from the foundation of the world" (Matt 25:34). Next the famous criteria for their reward are revealed (Matt 25:34–36):

I was hungry and you gave me food.

1. Culpepper, *Matthew*, 495.

I was thirsty and you gave me something to drink.

I was a *xenos*—foreigner, stranger—and you welcomed me.

I was naked and you gave me clothing.

I was sick and you took care of me.

I was in prison and you visited me.

For a Jewish listener at the time, most of this list would have been familiar. Food for the hungry, hospitality to the stranger, almsgiving to the needy, care for the sick. These were basic expressions of justice, mercy, and love. The idea that these are the kinds of behaviors that God cares about most resounds through the prophets (cf. Isa 58:6–11).

The reference to visiting those who are in prison is notable. It may be that this connects to the Jewish experience of bondage and exile in Babylon, or perhaps contemporary experiences under Roman and Herodian rule.

But the most striking thing about this text is the way the king/the Son of Man, identifies *himself* with the hungry, thirsty, stranger, naked, sick, and imprisoned. "I was hungry and you gave me food, I was thirsty and you gave me drink," and so on.

In Matt 25:37–40, the righteous, the ones who will inherit the kingdom, have no memory of encountering the king in their acts of mercy and justice. They have simply done the right thing for the human beings in need along the way. "When was it that we saw you hungry and gave you food, or thirsty and gave you something to drink?" The payoff line, the one that is so important to this moral teaching of Jesus, is of course this one: "Truly I tell you, just as you did it to one of the least of these brothers and sisters of mine, you did it to me" (Matt 25:40).

The passage then wends its inexorable way to the fierce coming judgment on those who have failed to provide care and mercy when the king came to them in the guise of the hungry, the thirsty, the stranger, the naked, the sick, and the imprisoned. Just as you did not help them, you did not help me. The judgment? Damnation.

There are three main traditions of interpretation of this teaching of Jesus.

The narrowest is that "the least of these" in this passage are the followers of Jesus, sent into the world on mission. Often persecuted and harassed, sometimes hungry and without shelter, these missionaries live in complete dependence on God and the hospitality of others. This reading of the passage suggests that the judgment of "the nations" hinges on their treatment of these missionaries. The main support for this interpretation is the full reading, "the least of these my brothers" (Matt 25:40; Gk: *adelphon*), as well as clues in the rest of Matthew.[2] This seems a cramped reading of the passage, at least for contemporary application.

Another interpretation is that the good people in the story are the "righteous gentiles." That is, the Jewish teacher Jesus is telling his Jewish listeners that those gentiles who act with justice and mercy and care to the needy are pleasing to God, even if they do not know anything about Torah or the God of Israel. Jesus would be saying that this is how "the nations," not the Jews, are to be judged. It would build on the very old Jewish idea that gentiles can be righteous, even pleasing to God, based on how they live. All humans are expected to meet a basic moral standard.

But the most inspiring reading also seems the most straightforward and most in keeping with the overall body of Jesus' moral teaching. There will be an eternal judgment for all humans, and it will be based on how we treat our fellow human beings, especially the most vulnerable and needy. It is this interpretation that has proven so inspiring to so many, and placed this text among the most significant of all Jesus' moral teachings.

If this is what Jesus was teaching, it places him squarely within the Jewish legal and prophetic tradition. The most striking thing about this passage remains the incarnational identification of the Judge of all the earth with the least of these. This is worth sitting with for a few moments.

There is some relevant OT background here. In Jewish thought an appointed messenger fully represented the sender. When God sent angels, the angels represented God. How people treated angels represented how they treated God. Consider the way that even today an ambassador fully represents the foreign sovereign who posts them. How we treat an ambassador equals how we treat the one who sent that ambassador.

In that sense, then, how we respond to the hungry, thirsty, stranger, naked, sick, and imprisoned people that we encounter is *ipso facto* how we respond to the one who sent them to us. (Which would also mean that God is the one who sends needy people to us!)

But we need to push further. In this story, the hungry, thirsty, etc., are not just representatives of God, or sent by God, they are God. Or, at least, God is incarnated in them. Jesus appears to be training believers through this story to see himself in the face of the suffering and needy people that

2. Culpepper, *Matthew*, 499–500, adopts this interpretation. In terms of the Gospel of Matthew in its original context, the "least of these" are the emissaries of Jesus on mission, and the nations are judged by how they have responded to them. But Culpepper acknowledges far broader interpretive possibilities.

we encounter. He doesn't just send them to us, like a king sending an ambassador. He *is* the suffering one. If you want to know where to find God incarnate in this world, look to the suffering ones.

Conclusion

The Radical Moral Message of Jesus

What is prized by humans is an abomination in the sight of God.
—LUKE 16:15

WE HAVE CAREFULLY CONSIDERED forty moral teachings of Jesus. Our question in this conclusion is whether these teachings add up to a single message. What did Jesus of Nazareth intend to say, overall? What was his moral message to the world? Here is my effort at a synopsis.

Even though we come from God our Creator, humanity is well and truly messed up. We look at the world and live our lives basically upside down, in a complete reversal of how we ought to think and live. We half-know this, but mainly deny it. This is where Jesus' moral message begins.

Jesus suggests that if we would watch and listen to our children and grandchildren, they could show us aspects of a better way. But we don't watch and listen to them. We instead ignore or even mistreat them, as we train them in our own messed-up values—so that when they grow up, they can fit in and succeed in the upside-down cultures that we have created.

Jesus understands with sympathy that humans are very needy creatures. We are not at fault in this; it is how we are made. We have daily physical needs that demand our attention. We can learn to discipline these somewhat, but they do make their demands felt. They also can create a gnawing sense of insecurity—especially if we must wonder where we will turn to find food to eat or a place to sleep, but that sense of anxiety can afflict absolutely anyone.

Jesus further understands that we are also needy emotional, relational, and spiritual creatures. These are the more interesting needs, because they are more uniquely human, and because the way we act to meet them can take such a great variety of forms—many of them fundamentally misguided or even destructive. Human life is in this sense a tragicomedy, in which we have a great many opportunities to watch ourselves and others flail around trying to get these needs met.

Trying to satisfy these needs drives many people much of the time into an array of sinful patterns of behavior. One characteristic human pattern is an unwillingness to discipline our basic physical neediness adequately. Another characteristic pattern is a tendency to look in the wrong places to get our hyped-up needs met. We often hurt ourselves and others this way.

Jesus clearly sees that one of the most interesting, subtle, and destructive "needs" that humans have is for status among our peers. Whether we call it honor (and contrast it with shame), status (and contrast it with marginality), or visibility (and contrast it with being invisible), human beings want to be recognized, want to be important, want to be valued. We also tend to treat honor, status, and visibility as zero-sum games, with more for us being less for others and vice versa. This is part of our moral sickness, that we are so competitive about such things. What a disastrous bondage this is for humanity.

Jesus knows that humans lie—a lot. We lie to God, to self, and to others. We lie because we can't stand the truth, can't face the truth, and are too embarrassed and proud to move beyond our posture of self-protection. We lie to ourselves about what really matters and what secures a good life. Building our houses on sand, we find our building projects unfinished or in ruins when we die, or when our world falls apart.

Jesus saw the significance of social practices. He saw that cultures reinforce these sinful human tendencies pretty much everywhere. Unfortunate basic tendencies (weaknesses) in our messed-up human nature get reinforced again and again by broadly accepted cultural patterns.

Essentially, what cultures do is teach us to build status around sinful human tendencies—which are reinforced rather than understood as sin. We honor the wealthy as better than the poor, the powerful as better than the powerless, those who live in luxury as better than those who are dirty or without homes, the adults as better than the children, the healthy as better than the sick, the physically strong as better than the weak, the kinfolk as better than the stranger, and so on.

It is when upside-down thinking like this, in family, neighborhood, music, art, economics, education, entertainment, religion, politics, and law, all reinforce each other, that the vast majority of human beings are taught and caught in patterns of valuing things that are an abomination to God. We have been trained away from true knowledge about ourselves, about what is real, about what matters.

Yes, that is exactly why Jesus said *"what is prized by humans is an abomination to God."* Our values are completely upside down. Human culture as we have set it up is a set of interconnected and idolatrous abominations to God that are celebrated by people—*the best people*—over endless generations!

To quote Paul (Rom 7:24): *Who will rescue us from this body of death?*

Our religion was and is supposed to help—from Jesus' very Jewish perspective, God spoke plenty clearly through the Law and the Prophets. But we humans often make a hash out of religion too.

Speaking in the tradition of the Jewish prophets, Jesus argued that many common *religious* patterns are adventures in missing the point. Celebrating wealth as reward from God, exploiting the poor and blaming them for their plight, treating illness as punishment from God, cooperating with unjust state officials and practices, honoring the high-born, focusing on minutiae rather than real human well-being, encouraging religiously prideful comparison with others, letting legalistic maneuvers reinforce sin, blessing nationalist violence and retaliation, undertaking showy acts of piety for human praise, participating in honor/shame-based reciprocity games, abandoning God's justice and love in the name of God himself . . . Jesus named it all.

Again, it seems that everything we value is upside down. What we think is awesome God thinks an abomination. What we think is great, God doesn't care about. The person we think is a nobody, God values. What we fear, God says shouldn't bother us.

We need to be stripped down, and to return to the basics. To the root (*radix*). We need *radical spiritual and moral surgery*. This is about more than morality. It begins with a theological vision and a spiritual practice that incorporate these things that Jesus taught us:

God is all and in all. God is the source of creation and life, the ground of existence, the destiny of the creation and of each of us.

God is King. God is the only King. God deserves our loyal service, far more than the earthly rulers whose showy pomp is a faint, idolatrous echo of the majesty of the one true King, and whose demands for loyalty God scorns. God requires and rightly deserves everything from us, his creatures.

God is love, offers love, requires love.

God wants justice, offers justice, requires justice, judges us on the basis of our justice.

God is fiercely sensitive to marginalized persons. They matter just as much to God as do the powerful ones. God seems radical that way but that's only because our moral vision is so messed up. Indeed, the last, least, and lost, is where we best meet God in the world.

God wants people to give their whole—full—complete—true—pure—hearts, selves, souls, and lives to him. This is way beyond rules and obedience. It's devotion. It's submission. It's love.

God wants people who are humble in heart, mournful over their sins and this screwed up world, hungry for justice, merciful and reconciling.

God wants people who will secure themselves by trusting in him rather than in foolish human strategies and schemes that are so constantly self-defeating.

Jesus' Way of living may feel like self-denial to us, perhaps especially at the beginning, when we first hear that call. But once we have learned to see Reality rightly, have reoriented our vision, it begins to feel more natural. As the world's illusions drop away, as the world's upside-downness becomes clearer, we become ready to turn ourselves right-side-up. Then we are not just willing but eager to learn how to do so.

God wants a radically reoriented humanity. But that begins with a vanguard group, the church, that will radically reorient in this Godward direction and who will fearlessly choose to play by God's rules, not by messed up human patterns. One day the will of God will be done in all the world. The "kingdom of God" is the name for a world turned right-side-up. The church is to be its first expression.

This kingdom of God has moral dimensions that can be practiced right now. Jesus is *not* just teaching high ideals or impossible ethical perfectionism intended to humble us by reminding us of how sinful and imperfect we are. We are that, for sure.

But this Way is about retraining. It is a retraining into practices Jesus taught, like peacemaking, forgiveness, economic simplicity, mercy, and generosity, turning the other cheek, enemy-love, covenant fidelity, truth telling, nonjudgmentalism, Good Samaritanism, standing with the vulnerable, valuing all people the same, leading by serving while not seeking human honor—it's a lovely way of life once you are in it, but it takes some training. The church is supposed to be where we get that training.

God truly honors heartfelt repentance, and we sure need to repent, not just once but often. Learning to see and act in the world in a way that completely reverses prevailing cultural patterns is very difficult. Backsliding is probably inevitable. We will need to repent, a lot.

The efforts that we make to turn the world's values upside down are likely to be met with opposition, from all centers of power—family, state, economy, religion, tradition, and culture. We feel that opposition within ourselves too. We might die in the effort to follow God this radically. But Jesus says this death, if it comes, is better than living falsely before God and hurting others as we get swept into corrupt ways of being.

Jesus the crucified was raised and now lives. His teachings are not a dead letter, but the ongoing message of the living Lord.

I believe that the teachings of Jesus offer the best ethical instruction, the best account of the will of God, that the world has ever heard.

I believe that Christians are those who commit to obey these teachings.

Blessed are those who bless the world by heeding and doing what Jesus taught.

Bibliography

Bibliowicz, Abel Mordecai. *Jewish-Christian Relations: The First Centuries*. N.p.: Mascarat, 2022.

Blount, Brian K., gen. ed. *True to Our Native Land: An African American New Testament Commentary*. Minneapolis: Fortress, 2007.

Bonhoeffer, Dietrich. *Discipleship*. Edited by Geoffrey B. Kelly and John D. Godsey. Minneapolis: Fortress, [1937] 2003.

Culpepper, R. Alan. *Matthew: A Commentary*. New Testament Library. Louisville: Westminster John Knox, 2021.

Davies, W. D. *The Setting of the Sermon on the Mount*. Cambridge: Cambridge University Press, 1964.

Davies W. D., and Dale C. Allison Jr. *Matthew*. Volume I:I–VII. International Critical Commentary. Edinburgh: T. & T. Clark, 1988.

De La Torre, Miguel. *The Politics of Jesús*. Lanham, MD: Rowman & Littlefield, 2015.

Edwards, James R. *The Gospel According to Mark*. Grand Rapids: Eerdmans, 2002.

Ford, David F. *The Gospel of John: A Theological Commentary*. Grand Rapids: Baker, 2021.

Gadenz, Pablo T. *The Gospel of Luke*. Catholic Commentary on Sacred Scripture. Grand Rapids: Baker Academic, 2018.

Garland, David E. *The NIV Application Commentary: Mark*. Grand Rapids: Zondervan, 1996.

Green, Joel B. *The Gospel of Luke*. New International Commentary on the New Testament. Grand Rapids: Eerdmans, 1997.

Gushee, David P. *Defending Democracy from Its Christian Enemies*. Grand Rapids: Eerdmans, 2023.

———. *Getting Marriage Right: Realistic Counsel for Saving and Strengthening Relationships*. Grand Rapids: Baker, 2004.

———. *Introducing Christian Ethics*. Canton, MI: Front Edge, 2022.

Gushee, David P., and Colin Holtz. *Moral Leadership for a Divided Age*. Grand Rapids: Brazos, 2018.

Gushee, David P., and Glen Harold Stassen. *Kingdom Ethics: Following Jesus in Contemporary Context*. 2nd ed. Grand Rapids: Eerdmans, 2017.

Harrison, Beverly Wildung. "The Power of Anger in the Work of Love." In *Making the Connections*, edited by Carol S. Robb, 3–21. Boston: Beacon, 1985.

Lapsley, Jacqueline, Carol A. Newsom, and Sharon H. Ringe, eds. *Women's Bible Commentary*. 3rd ed. Louisville: Westminster John Knox, 2012.

Levine, Amy-Jill *Short Stories of Jesus: The Enigmatic Parables of a Controversial Rabbi*. New York: HarperOne, 2015.

Levine, Amy-Jill, and Marc Zvi Brettler, eds. *The Jewish Annotated New Testament*. 2nd ed. New York: Oxford University Press, 2017.

Morris, Leon. *The Gospel According to John*. Rev. ed. The New International Commentary on the New Testament. Grand Rapids: Eerdmans, 1995.

Niebuhr, H. Richard. *Christ and Culture*. New York: Harper, 1951.

Niebuhr, Reinhold. *An Interpretation of Christian Ethics*. Louisville: Westminster John Knox, [1935] 2021.

Rauschenbusch, Walter. *The Social Principles of Jesus*. New York Grosset & Dunlap, 2016.

Sanders, E. P. *The Historical Figure of Jesus*. London: Penguin, 1993.

Secrest, Love Lazarus. *Race and Rhyme: Rereading the New Testament*. Grand Rapids: Eerdmans, 2022.

Solzhenitsyn, Aleksandr. *The Gulag Archipelago 1918–1956*. New York: Harper & Row, 1975.

Thompson, Marianne Meye. *John: A Commentary*. The New Testament Library. Louisville: Westminster John Knox, 2015.

Thurman, Howard. *Jesus and the Disinherited*. Boston: Beacon, [1949] 1996.

Wogaman, J., ed. *Readings in Christian Ethics: A Historical Sourcebook*. Louisville: Westminster John Knox, 1996.

Printed in Great Britain
by Amazon

47229379R00128